Korean Grammar
for Speaking
2

English Version

Song Won

Thanks to..

I would like to thank all of the people who have helped me publish this book, especially the English translators, Derrick Fernando Jaramillo Buxeda, Olivia Claire Crump, and Taylor Dawn Sandy, who did a wonderful proofreading job, my advisor Choi Yoon Sik, and my biggest supporter, Kim Hye Jeong, who has given me ideas, inspiration and very honest advice.
This book could have never been published without their help.

2018년 11월 10일
송 원

How to Study Languages?

When it comes to learning languages, how can we become multilingual? Can we teach ourselves? Is there a fast way? Is it necessary to go abroad to study a foreign language?

In the course of teaching myself several foreign languages I have realized a few things. I would like to share those lessons to provide some information with people who are interested in studying languages themselves.

Having an interest and love for the language you are learning is fundamental. With that you can gain knowledge easily. You should learn with passion, and wonder about many things. Get interested and have fun. Studying another language can be a tool to have fun, expose yourself to new experiences and ultimately, change your life.

Let's look at how to teach yourself a language more specifically:

1. Memorize the Characters

Obviously, you have to memorize the characters in order to read and write.

2. Study Grammar

If you are not trying to be a linguist, you don't necessarily have to study grammar terms like subject, object, etc., but you should learn how to conjugate. You should find the verb infinitives and conjugate them appropriately.

For example, in English, let's say you are studying the grammar rules for 'want to do something'. To make it work, you should add infinitives such as go, eat, study, etc. right after 'to'. Then you will make the sentences: "I want to go", "I want to eat", and "I want to study".
It's simple, right? From there you can begin to memorize words like 'he' and 'she' and swap them out with 'I' to make new sentences.

Korean, Japanese, Chinese and many other languages work the same way. Try to understand as simply as possible, so that you will be able to say whatever you want if you have the right words. You can make thousands of sentences if you learn proper grammar.

3. Memorize Words Everyday, little by little

Instead of memorizing 10-20 words all at once, I recommend memorizing the words around you one at a time.
Take an interest in things and situations around you and learn these words first. Put them in a portable device that you always have with you such as a cellphone. Use your free time, for example, waiting for the bus or riding the subway, to look at the words you entered whenever possible. It is also good to write the words on memo paper (like Post-it Notes) and stick them all around you. You can stick the words right next to your bed, on your desk, refrigerator, light switches, mirrors, closets, etc., so that you can always review these new words.

4. Study with Movies and TV Shows

Downloading a movie or a drama with subtitles is an easy way to be influenced by any language. First, pause what you are watching and read the subtitles out loud before an actor speaks, then play it and listen to what the actor says. Pause it again, and mimic the actor.
Repeat this a few times until you get used to it and feel like you are speaking just like the actor. By doing this, you are studying the accent and intonation that the actor has. It can be helpful to memorize and learn some words and expressions that you hear as well. Words you don't know can easily be searched on the internet.
Simply watching dramas and movies without practicing can be helpful too, but only when you are already familiar with the language.

5. Talk to Native Speakers

Talk with native speakers in person, over the phone, through texting or on a computer every day. If possible, make friends with native speakers who have the same interests as you. Use tools such as penpal websites, applications (I highly recommend using HelloTalk), voice calling, and video calling for chances to talk to them as much as you can. Social media outlets are not only for sharing your thoughts and pictures with your friends, but also can be useful tools to study languages. Many language exchange applications exist to reach native speakers of the language you are learning.

6. Meet Native Speakers

Memorizing words and studying grammar at your desk is not the only way to study languages.
Meet people, hang out with them, and spend time with them, too!
You should be exposed to the circumstances in which the language is used. Don't be shy even
though you have just started studying, and be confident even though you will make mistakes.
Use mistakes as another way of studying and take note when you make them. Review and correct the mistakes you made and try to use the correct language the next time.

7. Don't Ask Why

There are many questions you should ask when learning a language, for example, you should
ask if things are correct or not. But if you are not a linguist, and only want to speak, understand
and interact with other people in the language you are studying, don't ask why! It is not important to figure out why 'bag' is 'bag' in English for instance. Instead, focus your energy on what is
essential, the actual use of the language. If you are using the language correctly, keep using it.
If not, fix your mistakes. Irregulars? Memorize them!

8. Take the Language As It Is

Once you start learning a language you might have a habit of translating the language into your
mother tongue. Doing this is okay at the beginning, but it is not a good habit. Native speakers
would not read a book by translating it in their heads. Think of yourself as a native speaker
of your new language and try to read and understand and speak as they do. It won't be easy
at the beginning but you will get used to it and be able to speak and listen to native speakers
without translating.

9. Use the Circumstances Around You

Let's say there's a man walking outside, a girl is on the phone, another person is driving, and someone is drinking coffee.
Don't just walk away. Think about the situations in your head like "A man is walking", "A girl is talking on the phone with her friend" and see if you can describe these situations in the language you are studying.
Listen to what people are saying around you and think about how to say the phrases you hear in the language you are studying.
Everything that happens around you can be an opportunity to learn. In this way, you don't need to go abroad to study a language.

10. Simplify

You don't have to use big, difficult words. You don't have to try to find a perfectly matched word from your mother tongue. Instead, use simple words that you have learned and already know.

Don't forget that a great speaker is not a person who explains things with big words, but one who explains things using easy words that can be understood by people from age 10 to 100.

I hope these tips will help you as much as they helped me in learning new languages. Good luck and don't give up.

Thank you,

Steven Clemensen
TED 507
Dr. Cariaga
October 17, 2018

Language Autobiography

When I was in Korean class, it felt exciting to be a language learner because my Korean teacher made it feel attainable. He structured his lessons specifically for ex-pats living in Korea so that they could more easily and comfortably navigate their life. Most importantly, he made it clear that anybody can learn basic Korean through persistence and practice. Motivated to learn, I was working on my first homework assignment (writing the characters of Hangul, the Korean alphabet) at my new job at an English academy. My Korean boss, the director of the English academy, walked behind me and saw what I was working on. She gasped and quietly said, "Aheego. Oh my god… You have so far to go, you should just give up now." She may have been joking about my scribbly characters or perhaps the fact that I was an English teacher writing in Korean, but the damage was done. In that moment, I felt offended, discouraged, and that a connection with Koreans who spoke no English was unattainable. I felt the opposite of how my Korean teacher made me feel.

I realized that I now had two different types of educational influences is my life; one was a motivational educator (my Korean language teacher, named Song Won), who pushed my limits, cared about my passions and interests, and served as a role model for me as a teacher. The other was someone who ran a language academy who saw learning a new language from scratch as an impossible feat. I chose to follow the influence of the teacher that made me feel good, smart, and motivated. This motivation pushed me to learn how to read and write Hangul, and to speak and understand more Korean than my boss ever thought possible.

Song Won made me aware of my community cultural wealth, which is defined as "an array of knowledges, skills, abilities and contacts possessed and used by communities of color to survive and resist racism and other forms of oppression" (Yosso, 2005). (I realize that I am not a person of color, but while living in Korea, I was a minority and was navigating a society that was not built for me to succeed).

This is what ultimately turned this experience with my boss into something positive. Specifically, the capital I was able to use from my community cultural wealth was aspirational capital. This kept me focused on my hopes and dreams of learning Korean in the face of the challenges of living in a world that was completely foreign to me. I was able to latch onto this aspirational capital because my Korean teacher believed in me, pushed me out of my comfort zone, and would not accept excuses for my fears of failure or shyness. All of this motivated me to push through my fear and self-doubt and to take pride in my improvements, no matter how small.

Song Won also constantly pulled from my funds of knowledge, which is the inherent skills and knowledge that I have gained through my cultural and personal history (Moll, 1992). As an American who relocated to South Korea, he was wary of how this experience could be challenging and found ways to make my language learning experience useful in my personal life. To do this, he made sure to teach me how to speak about skateboarding. He taught me words and phrases that I could use with other Korean skaters. He did this so that I could meet more people, make more friends, and most importantly, learn more Korean. It worked. My life improved exponentially because he took the time to notice that skateboard culture was vital to my happiness. Through the skills he taught me, I was able to become deeply immersed in Korean culture.

These lessons had a profoundly positive effect on my life there, socially and professionally. I began to pull from my emergent bilingual students' funds of knowledge the next day by getting to know my students on a deeper level and what their hobbies, families, and dreams were. I continue practicing this today. I have also done my very best to make my students aware of their community cultural wealth through projects based around their cultures, dreams, hobbies, and families. I teach my students vocabulary, phrases, and slang that they can use in their personal life, with hopes that it will enrich their personal lives and help them reach their dreams. I also hold my students up to a high standard in order to push them to a level of success that exceeds their own expectations. I don't look at my students and laugh, like my boss. I set my students up for success, like Song Won.

Contents

Contents

Contents

나요?
(wonder if) (1)

No 받침 — 나요

가다 →	제주도에 어떻게 가나요?	비행기를 타고 가야 돼요.
go	I was wondering how to get to Jeju Island?	You have to go by plane.

사용하다 →	이 카메라를 어떻게 사용하나요?	저도 잘 모르겠어요.
use	I wonder how to use this camera?	I don't get it **either**.

받침 — 나요

키가 작다 →	(혹시) 그 여자는 키가 작나요?	작은 것 같아요.
short	I wonder if the woman is short?	I think she is short.

맞다 →	(혹시) 이 답이 맞나요?	아니요, 틀려요.
correct	I wonder if this answer is correct?	No, it's wrong.

Irregulars — ㄹ → 나요

팔다 →	이런 것은 어디에서 파나요?	인터넷에서 구할 수 있어요.
sell	I wonder where they sell something like this?	You can get it on the Internet.

날다 →	날개 **없이** 어떻게 나나요?	가능해요.
fly	I wonder how it flies **without** wings?	It's possible.

Connection

오다 →	오고 있나요?	[오다 + 고 있다 + 나요]
come	I wonder if you **are** coming?	

들어가다 →	들어가도 되나요?	[들어가다 + 도 되다 + 나요]
go in	I wonder if I **am allowed to** go in?	

신청하다 →	신청해야 되나요?	[신청하다 + 해야 되다 + 나요]
apply	I wonder if I **have to** apply?	

예약하다 →	예약할 수 있나요?	[예약하다 + ㄹ 수 있다 + 나요]
make a reservation	I wonder if I **can** make a reservation?	

Note

*'나요' can be used with adjectives and verbs.

*'나요' is also used when you are wondering about something to yourself.

But '요' should not to be included because you don't need to show respect to yourself.

Exercises Unit 1

1. Complete the blanks using '나요?'.

1) 있다   have, there is

2) 맞다   correct

3) 예약하다   book

4) 배달하다   deliver

5) 없다   don't have, there isn't

6) 물다   bite

7) 운전하다   drive

8) 영업하다   run a business

2. Complete the conversation using '나요?'.

있다	뜨겁다	영업하다	믿다	맞다	예약하다

1) 방을 어떻게 ____________ ?   저희 홈페이지에서 예약하시면 됩니다.

2) 혹시 여자친구가 ____________ ?   아니요. 저는 바빠서 여자친구를 만날 시간이 없어요.

3) 오늘 ____________ ?   네. 저희는 24시간 영업합니다. 배달도 하고요.

3. Complete the blanks using 'ㅆ다/었다/했다 + 나요?'.

1) 구하다   get, find out, obtain

2) 놓치다   miss

3) 끝나다   be finished

4) 알아듣다   understand, get

5) 마르다   dry

6) 잡다   catch, grab

7) 시작하다   begin, start

8) 이해하다   understand

4. Complete the conversation using 'ㅆ다/었다/했다 + 나요?'.

혼나다	늦다	알아듣다	끝나다	구하다	틀리다

1) 수업이 ____________ ?   네. 지금 나가요.

2) 제 말을 ____________ ?   아니요. 천천히 말씀해 주시겠어요?

3) 목걸이가 너무 예쁘네요. 어디에서 ____________ ?   인터넷에서 샀어요.

5. Complete the blanks using '야 되다/어야 되다/해야 되다 + 나요?'.

1) 납부하다   make a payment

2) 내다   pay, submit

3) 송금하다   send money

4) 결제하다   pay

5) 제출하다   submit

6) 입금하다   put money in an account

6. Complete the conversation using '야 되다/어야 되다/해야 되다 + 나요?'.

제출하다	알아듣다	예약하다	납부하다	결제하다

1) 이력서를 언제까지 ____________ ?   오늘까지 제출하셔야 돼요.

2) 핸드폰 요금을 한 달에 몇 번 ____________ ?   한 달에 한 번 납부하셔야 돼요.

3) 현금으로 ____________ ?   카드로 결제하셔도 돼요.

인가요?, ㄴ가요/은가요?
(wonder if) (2)

받침/No받침 — 인가요?

초보자 beginner	→	초보자인가요? I wonder if you are a beginner?

네. 저는 초보자예요.
Yes, I'm a beginner.

전문가 expert	→	전문가인가요? I wonder if you are an expert?

아니요. 저는 전문가가 아니에요.
No. I'm not an expert.

No받침 — ㄴ가요?

멋지다 stylish	→	제 가방이 멋진가요? I wonder if my bag is stylish?

괜찮네요.
Oh, it's alright.

이상하다 strange	→	제 목소리가 이상한가요? I wonder if my voice is strange?

아니요. 괜찮아요.
No. It's alright.

받침 — 은가요?

높다 high	→	63 빌딩이 높은가요? I wonder if the 63 building is high(tall)?

높죠!
Of course it's high(tall)!

낮다 low	→	제 한국어 수준이 낮은가요? I wonder if my Korean level is low?

아니요. 꽤 높은 것 같아요.
No. I think it's quite high.

Exception — ㄴ가요?

달다 sweet (taste)	→	너무 단가요? I wonder if it is too sweet?

괜찮은 것 같은데 조금 짜요.
I think it's okay, but a little salty.

운가요?

맵다 spicy	→	한국 음식이 매운가요? I wonder if Korean food is spicy?

아마 매울걸요?
It's probably spicy.

싱겁다 bland	→	음식이 조금 싱거운가요? I wonder if the food is bland?

아직 안 먹어 봤어요.
I haven't tried it yet.

Note

1. ㄴ/가요 is not used with verbs, and words that include 있다, 없다

2. ㄴ/가요 is also used when you are wondering about something to yourself.
But '요' should not be included because you don't need to show respect to yourself.

Exercises Unit 2

1. Complete the blanks using '-ㄴ가요?/은가요?'.

1) 짜다
salty

2) 맵다
spicy

3) 달다
sugary

4) 달콤하다
sweet (taste)

5) 시다
sour

6) 싱겁다
bland

7) 쓰다
bitter

8) 신선하다
fresh

2. Complete the conversation using '-ㄴ가요?/은가요?'.

신선하다 　　 짜다 　　 맵다 　　 낮다 　　 달다 　　 시다 　　 높다

A: 제가 비빔밥을 만들어 봤어요. 한 번 드셔 보세요.　　B: 고맙습니다. 잘 먹겠습니다.

A: 맛이 어때요? 조금 1)　　　　　?　　B: 네, 조금 매워요. 근데 괜찮아요. 먹을 수 있어요.

A: 다시 만들게요. 조금만 기다려 주세요.　　A: 어때요? 설탕을 넣었는데. 2)　　　　　?

B: 네. 너무 달아요.　　A: 그럼, 먹지 마세요.

3. Complete the blanks using '-ㄴ가요?/은가요?' or '-인가요?'.

1) 직장인
office worker

2) 활발하다
outgoing

3) 청순하다
innocent

4. Ask questions using '-ㄴ가요?/은가요?' or '-인가요?' and each of the words below.

1) (영국 사람, 미국 사람)

2) (대학생, 직장인)

3) (키가 크다, 키가 작다)

4) (활발하다, 조용하다)

5) (청순하다, 섹시하다)

5. You have a blind date. Ask your friend what you are wondering about the person using '-ㄴ가요?/은가요?' or '-인가요?'.

1)

2)

3)

4)

5)

UNIT 03 | ㄹ까요?/을까요?
(would?/might?)

일까요?

| 누구 | → | 누구일까요? | *누구일까요? shortened to 누굴까요? |
| who | | Who would it be? | |

| 연예인 | → | 연예인일까요? 아니면 일반인일까요? |
| celebrity | | Might she be a celebrity? If not, would she be an ordinary girl? |

No받침

ㄹ까요?

| 잘 어울리다 | → | 이 원피스가 저한테 잘 어울릴까요? |
| suit | | Might this dress suit me? |

| 좋아하다 | → | 제가 이 선물을 주면 그 사람이 좋아할까요? |
| like | | If I give this as a present, would he/she like it? |

받침

을까요?

| 작다 | → | 55 사이즈가 작을까요? 아니면, 너무 클까요? |
| small | | Might size 55 be small? If not, too big? |

| 맞다 | → | 66 사이즈가 맞을까요? |
| fit | | Would size 66 fit? |

Exception

ㄹ다 → 까요?

| 열다 | → | 오늘 휴일인데 가게가 문을 열까요? |
| open | | It's a holiday today, but might the store be open? |

ㅂ다 → 울까요?

| 맵다 | → | 한국 라면이 매울까요? 아니면, 중국 라면이 매울까요? |
| spicy | | Would Korean noodles be spicy? If not, would Chinese noodles be spicy? |

Note

ㄹ/을까요? is also used as 'shall we?'

ㄹ/을까요? is not used as 'would you?'

Exercises Unit 3

1. Complete the blanks using 'ㄹ까요?/을까요?' or '일까요?'.

1) 어른   adult

2) 아이   kid

3) 쉽다   easy

4) 어렵다   difficult

5) 크다   big

6) 작다   small

7) 팔다   sell

8) 맞다   correct, fit, get beaten

2. Complete the conversation using 'ㄹ까요?/을까요?'.

좋다	크다	팔다	어렵다	오다

1) A: 이 티셔츠를 인터넷에서 (　　　　)?　　　　　　　B: 글쎄요. 팔지 않을까요?

2) A: 스몰 사이즈가 저한테 (　　　　)?　　　　　　　B: 아니요. 안 클걸요. 딱 맞을 것 같아요.

3) A: TOPIK이 (　　　　)? 아니면 A LEVEL이 (　　　　)?　B: 당연히 A LEVEL이 어렵죠.

4) : 내일 비가 (　　　)? 안 (　　　)?　　　　　　　　B: 아마 올걸요?

5) : 이번 주말에 날씨가 (　　　)? 안 (　　　)?　　　　B: 잘 모르겠어요.

3. Make sentences using 'ㄹ까요?/을까요?' or '일까요?' and each of the words below.

1) (학생, 아저씨)

2) (한국인, 외국인)

3) (잘 어울리다, 안 어울리다)

4) (쉽다, 어렵다)

5) (열다, 닫다)

4. Make sentences using 'ㄹ까요?/을까요?'.

1)

2)

3)

4)

5)

ㄹ까 봐/을까 봐
(I think I will, so..)

No받침 — ㄹ까 봐

지**다**	→	질**까 봐**
lose		I think I wil lose, so

시합에서 질까 봐 걱정이 돼요.
I think I will lose the game, so I'm worried.

기다리**다**	→	기다릴**까 봐**
wait		I think you will wait, so

기다릴까 봐 일찍 나왔어요.
I thought you would wait for me, so I came out early.

걱정하**다**	→	걱정할**까 봐**
worry		I think you will worry, so

남자친구가 걱정할까 봐 안 갔어요.
I thought my boyfriend would worry , so I didn't go.

받침 — 을까 봐

죽**다**	→	죽**을까 봐**
die		I think I will die, so

죽을까 봐 도망갔어요.
I thought I would die, so I ran away.

젖**다**	→	젖**을까 봐**
get wet		I think I will get wet, so

비에 젖을까 봐 뛰었어요.
I thought I would get wet in the rain, so I ran.

맞**다**	→	맞**을까 봐**
be beaten		I think I will get beaten, so

형한테 맞을까봐 거짓말을 했어요.
I thought I would get beaten by my brother, so I lied.

Irregulars — ㄹ → 까 봐

물**다**	→	개가 물**까 봐** 못 만져요.
bite		I think the dog will bite me, so I can't touch it.

ㅂ → 울까 봐

춥**다**	→	날씨가 추**울까 봐** 자켓을 입었어요.
cold		I thought it would be cold, so I put on my jacket.

Connection

자다	→	자고 있을까봐 전화를 안 했어요.	[자다 + 고 있다 + 을까 봐]
sleep		I thought you would be sleeping, so I didn't call you.	

어렵다	→	못 할까 봐 걱정했는데 너무 잘해서 놀랐어요.	[못 + 하다 + ㄹ까 봐]
difficult		I was worried because I thought he couldn't do it, but he was too good, so I was surprised.	

Exercises Unit 4

1. Complete the blanks using '르까 봐/을까 봐'.

1) 들키다 ___________
get busted

2) 걸리다 ___________
get hooked

3) 떨어지다 ___________
fall down

4) 잊어버리다 ___________
forget

5) 잡히다 ___________
be caught

6) 놓치다 ___________
miss

7) 맞추다 ___________
set

8) 잃어버리다 ___________
lose

9) 혼나다 ___________
be scolded

10) 망치다 ___________
ruin

11) 망가뜨리다 ___________
break

12) 떨어뜨리다 ___________
drop

2. Answer the questions, and finish them using '르까 봐/을까 봐' with the given words, grammar.

잡히다	놓치다	덥다	떨어지다	잊어버리다

1) A: 왜 도망가요?　　　　　　　　B: 경찰한테 ___________

2) A: 왜 뛰었어요?　　　　　　　　B: 막차를 ___________

3) A: 왜 메모를 했어요?　　　　　　B: 회의 내용을 ___________

4) A: 왜 반바지를 입고 왔어요?　　B: 날씨가 ___________

5) A: 왜 밤을 새워서 공부해요?　　B: 중요한 시험에서 ___________

3. Complete the conversations using '르까 봐/을까 봐'.

떨어뜨리다	잃어버리다	늦다	혼나다	떨어지다

1) 지갑을 잃어버려서 엄마한테 ___________ 무서워서 집에 못 들어가고 있어요.

2) 제가 들고 있다가 ___________ 불안해서 못 들고 있겠어요.

3) ___________ 알람을 맞춰 놓고 잤는데 아침에 알람 소리를 못 들어서 결국에는 지각했어요.

4) 어릴 때 저희 엄마는 제가 가방을 ___________ 가방 앞에 제 이름을 크게 써 주셨어요.

5) 작년에 산 핸드폰의 가격이 ___________ 걱정이 돼서 팔았어요.

4. Make sentenses using '르까 봐/을까 봐'.

1) ___________

2) ___________

3) ___________

4) ___________

5) ___________

척하다 (체하다)
(pretend to)

Nouns — 인 척하다

남자친구	→	남자친구인 척하다	→	제 남자친구인 척해 주세요.
boyfriend		pretend to be a boyfriend		Please pretend to be my boyfriend (for me).
외계인	→	외계인인 척하다	→	외계인인 척했어요.
alien		pretend to be an alien		I pretended to be an alien.

Adjectives — ㄴ 척하다 / 은 척하다

예쁘다	→	예쁜 척하다	→	예쁜 척하지 마세요.
pretty		pretend to be pretty		Don't pretend to be pretty.
괜찮다	→	괜찮은 척하다	→	안 괜찮은데 괜찮은 척했어요.
alright		pretend to be alright		I am not alright, but I pretended to be alright.

Irregulars — ㅂ → 운 척하다

귀엽다	→	귀여운 척하다	→	귀여운 척하지 마세요.
cute		pretend to be cute		Don't pretend to be cute.

있다, 없다 → 는 척하다

멋있다	→	멋있는 척하다	→	멋있는 척하지 마세요.
cool, stylish		pretend to be cool		Don't pretend to be cool.

Verbs — 는 척하다

자다	→	자는 척하다	→	자는 척했어요.
sleep		pretend to sleep		I pretended to sleep.
듣다	→	듣는 척하다	→	듣는 척만 했어요.
listen		pretend to listen		I only pretended to listen.

Irregular — ㄹ → 는 척하다

알다	→	아는 척하다	→	아는 척하지 마세요.
know		pretend to know		Don't pretend to know.

Past — ㄴ 척하다 / 은 척하다

가다	→	간 척하다	→	안 갔는데 간 척했어요.
go		pretended I went		I didn't go, but I pretended I went.
먹다	→	먹은 척하다	→	점심을 안 먹었는데 먹은 척했어요.
eat		pretended I ate		I didn't have lunch, but I pretended I did have it.

1. Complete the blanks using 'ㄴ 척하다/은 척하다 + 지 마세요'.

1) 어리다
young

2) 멋있다
cool, stylish

3) 잘생기다
handsome

4) 괜찮다
alright

5) 잘나다
show-off

6) 지치다
be exhausted

2. Complete the sentences using the given words, and 'ㄴ 척하다/은 척하다 + 세요'. *도/어도: even if

잘생기다	어리다	괜찮다	배고프다	바쁘다	안 아프다

1) 나이가 많아도

2) 안 바빠도

3) 힘들어도

4) 배가 불러도

5) 못생겨도

6) 아파도

3. Complete the blanks using '는 척하다 + ㄹ 거예요'.

1) 못 알아듣다
can't understand

2) 모르다
don't know

3) 못 하다
can't do

4) 마음에 들다
like

5) 잘 못하다
not good at

6) 잘하다
do well (good at)

4. Complete the sentences using the given words, and '는 척하다 + 해야 돼요'.

모르다	없다	일하다	잘하다	못벌다	알다

1) 사장님이 들어 오시면

2) 한국어가 서툴러도

3) 비밀을 알아도

4) 정답을 몰라도

5) 돈이 많이 있어도

6) 돈을 많이 벌어도

5. Complete the blanks usingt 'ㄴ 척하다/은 척하다 + 했어요'.

1) 마음에 들다
like

2) 못 듣다
can't hear

3) 못 보다
can't see

4) 못 알아듣다
can't understand

5) 모르다
don't know

6) 잠이 들다
fall asleep

6. Complete the sentences using the given words, and 'ㄴ 척하다/은 척하다 + 했어요'.

못 알아듣다	못 듣다	못 보다

1) 이해했는데

2) 여자친구의 목소리를 들었는데

3) 길에서 전 남자친구를 봤는데

7. Make sentences using '척하다' with other grammar.

1)

2)

3)

UNIT 06 | (거의, 하마터면) ㄹ 뻔하다
(almost)

No 받침

ㄹ 뻔하다

다치다	→	다칠 뻔하다
get hurt		almost get hurt

(하마터면) 다칠 뻔했어요
I almost got hurt.

치이다	→	치일 뻔하다
get hit		almost get hit

어제 도로에서 차에 치일 뻔했어요.
I almost got hit by a car on the road yesterday.

받침

을 뻔하다

속다	→	속을 뻔하다
be deceived		almost be deceived

(하마터면) 사기꾼한테 속을 뻔했어요.
I was almost deceived by a scammer.

죽다	→	죽을 뻔하다
die		almost die

저는 1년 전에 오토바이에 치여서 죽을 뻔했어요.
I got hit by a motorcycle a year ago, so I almost died.

Irregular

ㄹ → 뻔하다

울다	→	울 뻔하다
cry		almost cry

영화가 너무 슬퍼서 울 뻔했어요.
The movie was too sad, so I almost cried.

Connection

큰일 나다	→	큰일 날 뻔하다
get in big trouble		almost get in big trouble

(하마터면) 큰일 날 뻔했는데 아무 일도 없었어요.
We almost got in big trouble, but nothing happened.

밟다	→	밟을 뻔하다
step on		almost step on

거북이를 밟을 뻔했는데 피했어요.
I almost stepped on a turtle, but I avoided it.

합격하다	→	합격할 뻔하다
pass (exam)		almost pass

시험에 합격할 뻔했는데 떨어졌어요.
I almost passed the test, but I failed.

Exercises Unit 6

1. Complete the blanks using '己 뻔했어요/을 뻔했어요'.

1) 속다
be deceived

2) 기절하다
pass out

3) 부딪치다
bump

4) 까먹다
forget

5) 떨어뜨리다
drop

6) 사고가 나다
have an accident

2. Create sentences with the given words using '己 뻔했다/을 뻔했다 + 는데'.

1) 속다

2) 죽다

3) 부딪치다

4) 떨어뜨리다

5) 사고가 나다

3. Complete the blanks using '己 뻔했어요/을 뻔했어요'.

1) 사기를 당하다
be scammed

2) 혼나다
be scolded

3) 쓰러지다
fall down

4) 넘어지다
fall

5) 실수하다
make a mistake

6) 후회하다
regret

7) 놓치다
miss

8) 쏟다
spill

9) 합격하다
pass (exams)

4. Create sentences with the given words using '己 뻔했다/을 뻔했다 + 는데'.

1) 쏟다

2) 놓치다

3) 실수하다

4) 합격하다

5) 사기를 당하다

5. Make sentences using '己 뻔하다/을 뻔하다'.

1)

2)

3)

4)

5)

기로
(decide to)

 — 기로 하다 —

돌아가**다**	→	돌아가**기로 하다**	내년 5월에 고향에 돌아가**기로 했어요.**
go back		decide to go back	I decid**ed** to go back to my hometown in May of next year.
담배를 끊**다**	→	담배를 끊**기로 하다**	오늘부터 담배를 끊**기로 했어요.**
quit smoking		decide to quit smoking	I decid**ed** to quit smoking from today.

[기로 하다 + 했다 + 고 = decid**ed** to do, and]

| 돈을 벌**다** | → | 돈을 벌**기로 하다** | 저는 공부하**기로 했고** 제 친구는 돈을 벌기로 했어요. |
| make money | | decide to make money | I decid**ed** to study, and my friend decided to make money. |

 — 기로 결정하다 = 기로 결심하다 —

*결정하다: make a decision, 결심하다, 마음먹다: make up one's mind

그만두**다**	→	그만두**기로 결정하다**	드디어 일을 그만두기로 결정했어요.
quit (working)		make a decision to quit	I **finally** made the decision to quit working.
배낭여행을 가**다**	→	배낭여행을 가**기로 결정하다**	저희는 결혼한 후에 배낭여행을 가기로 결정했어요.
go backpacking		make a decision to go backpacking	We made the decision to go backpacking after we get married.
유학가**다**	→	유학가**기로 결정하다**	유학가기로 결정했**는데** 부모님한테 말을 안 했어요.
study abroad		make a decision to study abroad	I made the decision to study abroad, but I didn't tell my parents.

 — 기로 약속하다 —

도와주**다**	→	도와주**기로 약속하다**	오늘 제 친구를 도와주기로 약속했어요.
lend a hand		promise to lend a hand	I promis**ed** to lend a hand to my friend today.
빚을 갚**다**	→	빚을 갚**기로 약속하다**	올해 3월**까지** 빚을 다 갚기로 약속했어요.
pay one's debt		promise to pay one's debt	I promised to pay my debt **by** March of this year.
만나뵙**다**	→	만나뵙**기로 약속하다**	1시에 선생님을 만나뵙기로 약속**해서** 지금 가야 돼요.
meet (formal)		promise to meet	I promised to meet my teacher at 1, so I have to go now.

Exercises Unit 7

1. Complete the blanks using '기로 하다 + 했어요'.

1) 구입하다
purchase

2) 그만두다
quit (job)

3) 이직하다
change jobs

4) 대신하다
replace

5) 휴직하다
leave of absence

6) 복직하다
return to work

2. Create sentences with the words given using '기로 하다 + 해서'.

1) 구입하다

2) 대신하다

3) 휴직하다

4) 복직하다

5) 이직하다

3. Complete the blanks using '기로 결정하다 + 했어요'.

1) 복수하다
revenge

2) 말을 놓다
talk in a casual way

3) 거래하다
make a deal

4) 이혼하다
get divorced

5) 약혼하다
get engaged

6) 결혼하다
get married

4. Create sentences with the words given using '기로 결정하다 + 했다 + 고'.

1) 말을 놓다

2) 약혼하다

3) 거래하다

4) 결혼하다

5) 이혼하다

5. Complete the blanks using '기로 약속하다 + 했어요'.

1) 돈을 갚다
pay one's debt

2) 버티다
endure / bear with

3) 돌보다
care

4) 정신을 차리다
get a grip

5) 노력하다
make an effort

6) 관리하다
manage

6. Create sentences with the words given using '기로 약속하다 + 했다 + 는데'.

1) 돌보다

2) 버티다

3) 돈을 갚다

4) 노력하다

5) 관리하다

던
(used to, was + ing, have + ed)

used to ——— 던 ———

좋아하다 + 사람 → 좋아하던 사람
like + person

person (I) used to like

그 사람은 제가 좋아하던 사람이에요.

He is the one I used to like.

살다 + 집 → 살던 집
live + house

house where (I) used to live

옛날에 제가 살던 집이에요.

It is the house where I used to live a long time ago (once upon a time).

was + ing ——— 던 ———

먹다 + 음식 → 먹던 음식 = 먹고 있던 음식
eat + food

food that I used to eat, food that I was eating

제가 자주 먹던 음식이에요.

It is a food that I used to eat often.

제가 조금 전에 먹던 음식이에요.

It is a food that I was eating a little while ago.

have + ed ——— 던 ———

좋아하다 + 사람 → 좋아했던 사람
like + person

person who (I) liked (don't like him/her anymore)

제가 좋아했던 사람이에요.

He is the one who I have liked.

살다 + 집 → 살았던 집
live + house

house where (I) have lived (don't live there anymore)

옛날에 제가 살았던 집이에요.

It is the house where I have lived a long time ago (once upon a time).

Exercises Unit 8

1. Complete the blanks using '던'.

1) 가다 + 곳 ___________
→ place where I used to go

2) 살다 + 데 ___________
→ place where I used to live

3) 쓰다 + 것 ___________
→ thing that I used to use

4) 팔다 + 물건 ___________
→ stuff that I used to sell

5) 일하다 + 회사 ___________
→ company that I used to work for

6) 사귀다 + 여자 ___________
→ a girl that I used to go out with

7) 다니다 + 교회 ___________
→ church that I used to go to

8) 사용하다 + 도구 ___________
→ tool that I used to use

2. Complete the conversations using '던'. (used to)

사귀다, 사람	일하다, 회사	다니다, 학교

1) A: 이곳은 제가 어릴 때 (　　　　　　)예요.　　　　B: 와, 진짜요? 엄청 크네요!

2) A: 여기는 아빠가 (　　　　　　)예요.　　　　B: 지금은 일을 안 하세요?

3) A: 제가 옛날에 (　　　　　　)한테 전화가 왔어요.　　　　B: 기분이 어땠어요?

3. Complete the conversations using '던'. (was + ing)

쓰다, 것	하다, 일	먹다, 것

1) A: 제가 (　　　　　　)인데 혹시 필요하세요?　　　　B: 주시면 감사하죠.

2) A: 제가 (　　　　　　)인데 먹고 싶으면 먹어도 돼요.　　　　B: 아, 괜찮아요. 안 먹을래요.

3) A: (　　　　　　)을 마저 하고 끝나면 연락해 주세요.　　　　B: 네. 빨리 끝낼게요.

4. Complete the conversations using '던'. (have + ed)

오다, 곳	살다, 아파트	다니다, 학원

1) A: 저기는 제가 초등학생 때 (　　　　　　)이에요.　　　　B: 지금은 안 다녀요?

2) A: 이 가게는 제가 옛날에 데이트할 때 자주 (　　　　　　)이에요.　　　　B: 그대로예요?

3) A: 저 아파트는 10년 전에 부모님이 (　　　　　　)예요.　　　　B: 많이 변했나요?

5. Make sentences using '던'.

1) ___________

2) ___________

3) ___________

UNIT 09 | 쓰었다/었었다/했었다
(used to)

였었다/이었었다

백만장자 → 백만장자**였었다**　　제 친구의 이모는 백만장자였었어요.
millionaire　　used to be a millionaire　　My friend's aunt used to be a millionaire.

스무 살 → 스무 살**이었었다**　　A: 저도 한 때는 스무 살이었었어요.
twenty years old　　used to be 20　　Once, I used to be 20 too.

No받침

쓰었다

가**다** → 갔**었다**　　중학생 때 가끔 피씨방에 갔었어요.
go　　used to go　　I sometimes used to go to the Internet cafe
　　when I was a middle school student.

비싸**다** → 비쌌**었다**　　1년 전에 엄청 비쌌었는데 지금은 안 비싸네요.
expensive　　used to be expensive　　It used to be really expensive, but it's not expensive now.

받침

었었다

읽**다** → 읽**었었다**　　대학생 때 항상 책을 읽었었어요.
read　　used to read　　I always used to read books when I was a university student.

돈을 벌**다** → 돈을 벌**었었다**　　젊을 때 돈을 많이 벌었었어요.
make money　　used to make money　　I used to make a lot of money when I was young.

하다

했었다

좋아**하다** → 좋아**했었다**　　옛날에 동물을 좋아했었어요.
like　　used to like　　I used to like animals once upon a time.

일**하다** → 일**했었다**　　호주에 있을 때 편의점에서 일했었어요.
work　　used to work　　I used to work at a convenience store when I was in Australia.

Irregular　　Follow the present tense format

오**다** → 왔**었다**　　어릴 때 이 가게에 자주 왔었어요.
come　　used to come　　I used to come to this store often when I was young.

Exercises Unit 9

1. Complete the blanks using '씼었다/었었다/했었다 + 어요'.

1) 다니다
attend, go

2) 사귀다
go out with

3) 평범하다
ordinary

4) 근무하다
work

5) 신중하다
careful

6) 고집이 세다
stubborn

7) 꼼꼼하다
meticulous

8) 알바하다
do the part-time job

9) 잘하다
good at

10) 털털하다
easy-going (personality)

11) 소심하다
timid

12) 까다롭다
picky

2. Complete the sentences using 'ㄹ 때/을 때', and '씼었다/었었다/했었다 + 어요'.

1) (유치원에 다니다 / 사귀다)

2) (스무 살 / 잘하다)

3) (어리다 / 고집이 세다)

4) (사업하다 / 돈을 벌다)

5) (젊다 / 인기가 많다)

3. Complete the sentences using '씼었다/었었다/했었다 + 는데'.

까다롭다	많다	잘하다	유명하다	못 먹다

1) 옛날에는 __________ 요즘에는 나이를 먹어서 못해요.

2) 어릴 때는 좋아하는 것이 __________ 지금은 좋아하는 것이 없어요. *것이 shortened to 게

3) 원래 성격이 되게 __________ 어른이 되니까 털털해지고 평범해졌어요.

4) 한 십 년전에는 __________ 지금은 아무도 몰라요.

5) 처음에는 회를 __________ 지금은 잘먹어요.

4. Think about your past, and write about what you used to be, do, etc using '씼었다/었었다/했었다'.

1)

2)

3)

4)

5)

던데요?
(I've done it, **but** it was)

 ---------------------- 던데요/이던데요 ----------------------

별로 → 별로**던데요**
not really

A: 무선 청소기가 좋아요.　　　　　　　　B: (제가 사용해 봤는데) 별로던데요?

The wireless vacuum is good.　　　　　　(I've used it, but) It was not really good?

천 원 → 천 원**이던데요**
1,000 won

A: 이것은 만 원이었어요.　　　　　　　　B: (제가 봤는데) 천 원이던데요?

This thing was 10,000 won.　　　　　　　(I've seen it, but) It was 1,000 won?

 ---------------------- 던데요 ----------------------

성실하다 → 성실하**던데요**
be diligent

A: 그 사람은 항상 지각해요.　　　　　　B: (제가 지켜봤는데) 성실하던데요?

He/she is always late.　　　　　　　　　(I've kept an eye on him, but) He/she is diligent?

좋다 → 좋**던데요**
be good

A: 이 제품은 안 좋아요.　　　　　　　　B: 그래요? (제가 써 봤는데) 좋던데요?

This product is not good.　　　　　　　Is it? (I've used it, but) It was good?

 ---------------------- 던데요 ----------------------

가다 → 가**던데요**
go

A: 혹시 케이트 씨를 봤어요?　　　　　　B: 네. (제가 봤는데) 저쪽으로 가던데요?

I wonder if you've seen Miss Kate?　　　Yes. (I've seen her, but) She was going that way?

놀다 → 놀**던데요**
hang out

A: 제 아들은 친구랑 놀고 있어요.　　　　B: (제가 봤는데) 혼자 놀던데요?

My son is hanging out with his friends.　(I've seen him, but) He was hanging out alone?

A: 매니저님, 교수님 오셨죠?　　　　　　B: (확인해 봤는데) 아직 안 오셨던데요?

Manager, the professor came, right?　　(I've checked, but) He hasn't come yet?

A: 학생들이 경주에 가고 싶어해요.　　　B: (물어봤는데) 보라카이에 가고 싶어 하던데요?

Students want to go to GyeongJoo.　　　(I've asked them) They want to go to Boracay?

1. Complete the blanks using '던데요?'.

1) 순하다
mild

2) 사납다
wild

3) 정직하다
honest

4) 청순하다
innocent

5) 알다
know

6) 모르다
don't know

7) 복잡하다
be complicated

8) 순진하다
naive

2. Answer the questions using '던데요?'.

| 사납다 | 알다 | 정직하다 | 비가 내리다 | 학교에 있다 |

1) A: 제 강아지는 아주 순해요.   B:

2) A: 그 사람은 거짓말을 잘해요.   B:

3) A: 엄마는 모르세요.   B:

4) A: 오늘 날씨가 좋으니까 놀이공원에 갈까요?   B:

5) A: 지수는 지금 어디에 있어요?   B:

3. Complete the blanks using '고 있다' + '던데요?'. (I saw him/her doing something.)

1) 청소하다
clean

2) 숙제하다
do homework

3) 정리하다
arrange

4) 치우다
tidy up

5) 올라가다
go up

6) 내려가다
go down

7) 기다리다
wait

8) 훔쳐보다
peep

9) 올리다
upload

4. Answer the questions using '고 계시다' + '던데요?'.

1) A: 삼촌, 고모는 뭐 하고 계세요?   B:

2) A: 고모, 이모는 어디에 계세요?   B:

3) A: 큰아버지, 큰어머니를 보셨어요?   B:

4) A: 고모부, 이모부는 지금 일하고 계시죠?   B:

5) A: 장모님, 장인어른은 지금 쉬고 계시죠?   B:

5. Create conversations using '던데요?'.

1) A: B:

2) A: B:

3) A: B:

4) A: B:

5) A: B:

더라고요
(I've done it, **and** actually it is/was)

Nouns ──────────── 더라고요, 이더라고요 ────────────

별로 → 별로더라고요.
not really

제가 그 이어폰을 사용해 봤는데 별로더라고요.
I've used those earphones, and they were not really good.

화요일 → 화요일이더라고요.
Tuesday

오늘 월요일인 줄 알았는데 확인해 보니까 화요일이더라고요.
I thought today was Monday, but I've checked, so it's actually Tuesday.

No받침/받침 ──────────── 더라고요 ────────────

신기하다 → 신기하더라고요.
be amazed
(unreal)

어제 처음으로 불꽃놀이를 봤는데 엄청 신기하더라고요.
I saw fireworks for the first time yesterday, and it was really amazing.

상태가 좋다 → 상태가 좋더라고요.
in a good condition

(제가 확인해 봤는데) 상태가 좋더라고요.
(I've checked it, and) It is in a good condition.

No받침/받침 ──────────── 더라고요 ────────────

따라오다 → 따라오더라고요.
follow

오늘 어떤 남자가 저를 따라오더라고요.
(I've seen the man, and) He was following me today.

마음에 들다 → 마음에 들더라고요
like

(생각해 봤는데) 빨간색이 제일 마음에 들더라고요.
(I've thought about it, and) I like the red one the most.

Exercises Unit 11

1. Complete the blanks using '더라고요/이더라고요'.

1) 긍정적
positive

2) 부정적
negative

3) 감동적
touching (emotions)

4) 부드럽다
be soft

5) 부끄럽다
be ashamed

6) 어울리다
suit

7) 부럽다
envy

8) 헷갈리다
be confused

9) 평화롭다
peaceful

2. Complete the conversations using '더라고요/이더라고요' with the given words.

| 감동적 | 부럽다 | 헷갈리다 | 긍정적 | 평화롭다 |

1) A: 시골에 가 봤어요? B: 네. 가 봤는데 엄청

2) A: 영화 '너의 이름은'을 봤어요? B: 네. 얼마 전에 여자친구랑 봤는데

3) A: 제 친구가 결혼을 했는데 너무   . B: 부러워하지 마세요. 힘들어요.

4) A: 그 남자를 만났죠? 어땠어요? B: 사람이 되게

5) A: 영어랑 일본어는 정말 쉬운 것 같아요. B: 진짜요? 저는 조금

3. Connect the conversations correctly.

1) A: 여름 방학에 시골에 다녀왔는데   •   • 1) 차가 많이 막히더라고요.

2) A: 죄송해요. 제가 조금 늦었죠?   •   • 2) 공기도 좋고, 조용하고, 평화롭더라고요.

3) A: 나갈 때 우산을 가지고 가세요.   •   • 3) 너무 부정적이더라고요.

4) A: 저 가게에서 파는 아이스크림을 먹어 봤는데 •   • 4) 부드럽더라고요.

5) A: 제가 그 여자랑 얘기한 적이 있는데   •   • 5) 밖에 비가 오더라고요.

4. Complete the sentences using '더라고요' with the given grammar and words.

1) 12시에 도착했는데 콘서트가 이미   (끝나다 + ㅆ다 + 더라고요)

2) 제가 알아봤는데 이벤트에 참여하고 싶으면 회원으로   (가입하다 + 해야 되다 + 더라고요)

3) 어제 밤에 베트남에 관한 다큐멘터리를 봤는데   (가다 + 고 싶다 + 더라고요)

4) 지하철에서 고등학교 동창을 만났는데 웹툰을   (보다 + 고 있다 + 더라고요)

5) 그 신발을 사고 싶었는데 너무   (비싸다 + ㄴ 것 같다 + 더라고요)

UNIT 12 | (심지어) 도/어도/해도
(even)

Nouns — 도

아이들	→	A: 어떻게 알았어요?	B: (심지어) 아이들도 다 알아요.
children		How did you know?	Even children know it all.

교수님	→	A: 교수님께 여쭈어 보세요.	B: (심지어) 교수님도 몰라요.
professor		Try to ask the professor.	Even my professor doesn't know.

No받침 — 도

느리다	→	A: 버스가 너무 느리네요.	B: 느려도 괜찮아요.
be slow		Oh, the bus is too slow.	It is okay even though it's slow.

화나다	→	A: 진짜 화나요.	B: 화나도 참으세요.
be angry		I'm really angry.	Calm down even though you are angry.

받침 — 어도/아도

늦다	→	A: 벌써 12시예요.	B: 늦어도 안 혼나요.
be late		It's already 12 o'clock.	I don't get scolded even if I'm late.

밀다	→	A: 힘껏 밀어 보세요.	B: 힘껏 밀어도 안 움직여요.
push		Try to push it with all your strength.	It doesn't move even though I push it with all my strength.

하다 — 해도

말하다	→	A: 힘들면 남자친구한테 말하세요.	B: (아무리) 말해도 몰라요. (No matter how many times) He doesn't get it even though I tell him.
say, tell		Tell your boyfriend if it's hard.	

설득하다	→	A: 아버지를 설득해 봤어요?	B: (아무리) 설득해도 안 들어요. (No matter how many times) He doesn't listen even though I try to persuade him.
persuade		Have you ever persuaded your father?	

Irregular — Follow the present tense format

춥다	→	A: 너무 추워요.	B: 추워도 참으세요.
cold		It's too cold.	Please be patient even though it's cold.

Connection

사다	→	사고 싶어도 못 사요.	[사다 + 고 싶다 + 어도]
buy		I can't buy it even if I want to.	
	→	살 수 있어도 안 살 거예요.	[사다 + ㄹ 수 있다 + 어도]
		I'm not going to buy it even if I can.	

Exercises Unit 12

1. Complete the blanks using '도/어도/해도'.

1) 울다
cry

2) 조르다
pester

3) 빌다
beg

4) 주다
give

5) 돈을 벌다
make money

6) 느리다
slow

7) 어렵다
difficult

8) 안 되다
doesn't work

9) 노력하다
effort

10) 졸리다
sleepy

11) 괴롭다
painful

12) 게으르다
lazy

2. Finish the sentences using '도/어도/해도' with the given words.

1) ___________ 갈게요.

2) 조금 ___________ 괜찮아요.

3) 돈 없이 ___________ 행복할 수 있어요.

4) 여자친구가 ___________ 외로워요.

5) 10년을 ___________ 안 되네요.

| 비가 내리다 |
| 느리다 |
| 살다 |
| 있다 |
| 노력하다 |

6) ___________ 오늘까지 해야 돼요.

7) 아무리 ___________ 용서 못 해요.

8) 아무리 ___________ 안 줄 거예요.

9) 잘 ___________ 포기하지 마세요.

10) 힌트를 ___________ 못 맞혀요.

| 어렵다 |
| 빌다 |
| 조르다 |
| 안 되다 |
| 주다 |

3. Complete the conversations using '도/어도/해도' and the given words.

| 없다 | 기분이 나쁘다 | 늦다 | 죽다 | 잘해 주다 |

1) A: 죄송합니다. 차가 막혀서 조금 늦을 것 같아요. B: ___________ 괜찮으니까 천천히 오세요.

2) A: 지금 제 통장에 1,300원밖에 없어요. B: 돈이 다가 아니에요. 돈이 ___________ 행복할 수 있어요.

3) A: 후배가 먼저 승진을 해서 기분이 나빠요. B: ___________ 어쩔 수가 없어요. 더 노력해 보세요.

4) A: 제가 맨날 챙겨주고 잘해 줬는데.. B: 제가 뭐라고 했어요. 아무리 ___________ 소용이 없다니까요.

5) A: 잊을 수 있어요? B: ___________ 못 잊어요.

4. Make sentenses using '도/어도/해도'.

1) ___________

2) ___________

3) ___________

4) ___________

5) ___________

UNIT 13 | ~지도 않다, ~지도 못하다
(don't even, not even, can't even)

Nouns — 도 (마저, 조차)

10원	→	A: 저는 돈이 없어요.	B: (심지어) 10원도 없어요?
penny		I don't have money.	You don't even have a penny?

행사	→	A: 행사가 시작됐어요.	B: 아직 6시도 아닌데 벌써 시작했어요?
event		The event has started.	It's not even 6 o'clock yet, but has it already started?

No받침 — 지도

친하다	→	A: 친하지도 않은데 왜 도와줬어요?	B: 불쌍하잖아요...
be close		You are not even close with him, but why did you help him?	You know he is pathetic...

나가다	→	무서워서 나가지도 못 했어요.	B: 무슨 일이라도 생겼어요?
go out		I was scared, so I couldn't even go out.	Did something happen?

받침 — 지도

알다	→	A: 다 알아요.	B: 알지도 못하면서 아는 척하지 마세요.
know		I know everything.	You don't even know, so don't pretend to know.

벗다	→	A: 남편은 뭐 하고 있어요?	B: 양말을 벗지도 않고 자고 있어요.
take off		What is your husband doing?	He didn't even take off his socks and he's sleeping.

하다 — 도/지도

환전하다	→	1. 내일 일본에 가는데 환전도 못했어요.	2. 내일 일본에 가는데 환전하지도 못했어요
exchange money		I will go to Japan tomorrow, but I didn't even exchange money.	I will go to Japan tomorrow, but I didn't even exchange money.

기대하다	→	1. 기대도 안 해요.	2. 기대하지도 않아요.
expect		I don't even expect (anything).	I don't even expect (anything).

Connection

끝내다	→	숙제를 다 끝내지도 않고 나갔어요.	[끝내다 + 지도 않다 + 고]
finish		He didn't even finish all his homework, and went out.	

하다	→	하지도 못하면서 왜 한다고 했어요?	[하다 + 지도 못하다 + 면서]
do		You can't even do it, but why did you say you will do it?	

1. Complete the blanks using '지도 않다'.

1) 부럽다 ____________
envy

2) 부끄럽다 ____________
be embarrassed

3) 건드리다 ____________
touch

4) 떨다 ____________
shake (nervous)

5) 도망가다 ____________
run away

6) 익숙하다 ____________
be used to it, familiar

7) 지겹다 ____________
be sick and tired

8) 생각하다 ____________
think

9) 인정하다 ____________
admit

2. Translate the sentences using the grammar that are used with '지도 않다'.

1) ____________ ?
Are you not even sick and tired of it?

5) ____________ .
I didn't even touch it.

2) ____________ .
They don't even admit it.

6) ____________ !
Oh, she doesn't even shake!

3) ____________ ?
Are you not even embarrassed?

7) ____________ .
I didn't even think.

4) ____________ .
I'm not even used to it.

8) ____________ ?
Don't you even envy her?

3. Make sentences using '지도 않다'.

1) ____________

2) ____________

3) ____________

4) ____________

5) ____________

4. Complete the blanks using '지도 못하다'.

1) 말하다 ____________
say

2) 꿈을 이루다 ____________
achieve a dream

3) 떠들다 ____________
make noise

4) 움직이다 ____________
move

5) 가입하다 ____________
join (become a member)

6) 탈퇴하다 ____________
leave (the group)

7) 표현하다 ____________
express

8) 손톱을 깎다 ____________
clip one's nails

9) 발톱을 깎다 ____________
cut one's toenails

5. Make sentences using '지도 못하다'.

1) ____________

2) ____________

3) ____________

4) ____________

5) ____________

(아무리) 더라도
(even if)

Nouns ········ 더라도/이더라도 ········

친구	→	친구더라도
friend		even if he is your friend

(아무리) 친한 친구더라도 용서 못 해요.
Even if she is a close friend, I can't forgive her.

교수님	→	교수님이더라도
professor		even if he is a professor

교수님이더라도 그렇게 행동하면 안 돼요.
Even if he is a professor, he shouldn't act like that.

No받침 ········ 더라도 ········

비싸다	→	비싸더라도
expensive		even if it's expensive

(아무리) 비싸더라도 필요하면 사세요.
Even if it is expensive, buy it if you need it.

떠나다	→	떠나더라도
leave		even if I leave

제가 떠나더라도 슬퍼하지 마세요.
Even if I leave, please don't be sad.

받침 ········ 더라도 ········

힘들다	→	힘들더라도
hard		even if it's hard

(아무리) 힘들더라도 포기하면 안돼요.
Even if it is hard, you shouldn't give up.

없다	→	거기에 없더라도
not to be		even if I'm not there

제가 거기에 없더라도 외로워하지 마세요.
Even if I'm not there, Please don't be lonely.

Connection

갖고 싶다	→	(아무리) 갖고 싶더라도 훔치면 안 돼요.	[갖다 + 고 싶다 + 더라도]
want to have		(No matter how much) Even if you want to have it, you shouldn't steal it.	

하기 싫다	→	하기 싫더라도 참고 해 보세요.	[하다 + 기 싫다 + 더라도]
don't want to do		Even if you don't want to do it, be patient and try it.	

없다	→	전에 해 본 적이 없더라도 해야 돼요.	[해 본 적이 없다 + 더라도]
don't have		Even if you haven't done it before, you have to do it.	

Exercises Unit 14

1. Complete the blanks using '더라도'.

1) 외롭다
lonely

2) 그립다
miss

3) 쑥스럽다
shy

4) 자존심이 상하다
hurt one's pride

5) 힘들다
hard

6) 귀찮다
don't feel like doing it

7) 이용하다
use

8) 답답하다
frustrated

9) 지겹다
sick and tired

10) 화가 나다
angry

11) 헤어지다
break up

12) 실패하다
fail

2. Complete the conversations using '더라도', and the given words.

귀찮다	쉽다	자존심이 상하다	힘들다	화가 나다

1) A: 시험 문제가 아무리   방심하지 마세요.   B: 네. 걱정하지 마세요. 최선을 다할게요.

2) A: 먼저 사과하세요.   B: 제 잘못이 아니라니까요.

3) A: 아무리   복습을 해야 돼요.   B: 아, 하기 싫다고요.

4) A: 물건을 던지면 안 돼요.   B: 네...

5) A: 일이 조금   좋은 기회라고 생각하고 최선을 다하세요.

3. Make conversations using '더라도' and the given words.

외롭다	실패하다	쑥스럽다	없다	답답하다

1) A: B:

2) A: B:

3) A: B:

4) A: B:

5) A: B:

4. Make sentences using '더라도'.

1)

2)

3)

4)

5)

UNIT 15 | (갑자기)더니
(Suddenly) It happened, and then...

멈추**다**	→	갑자기 버스가 멈추**더니** 운전 기사가 내렸어요.
stop		All of a sudden the bus stopped, and then the driver got off.
내리**다**	→	운전 기사가 내리**더니** 담배를 피우기 시작했어요.
get off		The bus driver got off, and then started smoking.
담배를 피우**다**	→	담배를 피우**더니** 한숨을 쉬었어요.
smoke		He smoked, and then sighed.

손을 들**다**	→	한 학생이 갑자기 손을 들**더니** 일어섰어요.
raise one's hand		A student suddenly raised his hand, and then stood up .
울**다**	→	갑자기 울**더니** 집에 가고 싶다고 말했어요.
cry		He suddenly cried, and then said that he wanted to go home.
떨**다**	→	몸을 떨**더니** 쓰러졌어요.
shake (body)		His body shook, and then he fell down (pass out).

		[먹다 + 었다 + 더니]
먹다	→	점심을 너무 많이 먹었더니 아직도 배가 불러요.
eat		I had too much lunch, then I'm still full.
		[가다 + 야 되다 + ㄴ다고 하다 + 더니]
전화하다	→	가야 된다고 하더니 아직 안 갔어요?
call		You said you have to go, but then you still didn't leave?
		[떠나다 + 고 싶다 + 어 하다+ 더니]
떠나다	→	그렇게 도시를 떠나고 싶어 하더니 결국 시골로 떠났네요.
leave		He wanted to leave the city so bad, so then he left to the country side in the end.

When 더니 is attached to another conjugation, it does not carry the meaning of 'suddenly'.

Exercises Unit 15

1. Complete the blanks using '더니'.

1) 세우다
make something stand, stop

2) 일어서다
stand up

3) 흔들리다
be shaken (stuff)

4) 부르다
call (someone)

5) 들어오다
come in

6) 흐려지다
get cloudy

7) 멈추다
stop

8) 꺼지다
be turned off

9) 건너다
cross (road)

10) 소리를 지르다
shout

11) 떨어지다
be dropped

12) 다가오다
come close

2. Complete the sentences using '더니'.

일어서다	다니다	소리를 지르다	꺼지다	멈추다

1) A: 무슨 일이에요?　　　　　　　　　　B: 갑자기 엘리베이터가 　　　　　　불이 꺼졌어요.

2) A: 무슨 일로 오셨어요?　　　　　　　　B: 갑자기 핸드폰이 　　　　　　다시 안 켜져요.

3) A: 데릭 씨가 학원에 　　　　　한국어 실력이 더 좋아졌어요.　B: 와, 열심히 하시나 봐요.

4) A: 학생이 자리에서 　　　　　화장실로 뛰어 갔어요.　B: 왜요?

5) A: 왜 싸웠어요?　　　　　　　　　　B: 저 사람이 먼저 저한테 　　　　　　화를 냈어요.

3. Complete the sentences using '더니, 기 시작했어요' and the words given.

1) 공원에서 산책을 하고 있었는데 갑자기 하늘이 　　　　　　　　[흐려지다, 비가 내리다]

2) 방에서 게임을 하고 있었는데 갑자기 엄마가 　　　　　　　　[들어 오시다, 소리를 지르다]

3) 학교에 가고 있었는데 외국인이 저한테 　　　　　　　　[다가오다, 영어로 질문하다]

4) 집에서 드라마를 보고 있었는데 갑자기 건물이 　　　　　　　　[흔들리다, 물건들이 떨어지다]

5) 횡단보도를 건너고 있었는데 갑자기 어떤 남자가 　　　　　　　　[차를 세우다, 다가오다]

4. Make sentences using '더니'.

1)

2)

3)

4)

5)

지다/어지다/해지다
(become, get)

No 받침 ┄┄┄┄┄┄┄┄┄┄┄┄┄┄ 지다 ┄┄┄┄┄┄┄┄┄┄┄┄┄┄

싸**다**	→	싸**지다**
cheap		**become** cheap

최근에 금이 싸졌어요.
Gold **became** cheap recently.

비싸**다**	→	비싸**지다**
expensive		become expensive

요즘 채소가 너무 비싸졌어요.
Vegetables became too expensive these days.

받침 ┄┄┄┄┄┄┄┄┄┄┄┄┄┄ 어지다 / 아지다 ┄┄┄┄┄┄┄┄┄┄┄┄┄┄

길**다**	→	길**어지다**
long		get long

속눈썹이 더 길어졌네요!?
Oh, your eyelashes got longer!?

작**다**	→	작**아지다**
small		get small

컴퓨터 화면이 더 작아진 것 같아요.
I think the computer screen got smaller.

하다 ┄┄┄┄┄┄┄┄┄┄┄┄┄┄ 해지다 ┄┄┄┄┄┄┄┄┄┄┄┄┄┄

우울**하다**	→	우울**해지다**
depressed		get depressed

갑자기 우울해져서 아무것도 하기 싫어요.
I got depressed all of sudden, so I don't want to do anything.

깨끗**하다**	→	깨끗**해지다**
clean		get clean

방이 깨끗해졌네요!?
Oh, the room got cleaned!?

Irregulars ┄┄┄┄┄┄┄┄┄┄┄┄┄┄ Follow present tense format ┄┄┄┄┄┄┄┄┄

어둡**다**	→	어두**워지다**	낫**다**	→	나**아지다**	크**다**	→	커**지다**
dark		get dark	better		get better	big		get bigger

게으**르다**	→	게을**러지다**	예쁘**다**	→	예뻐**지다**	바쁘**다**	→	바빠**지다**
lazy		become lazy	pretty		became pretty	busy		get busy

Exercises Unit 16

1. Complete the blanks using '지다/어지다/해지다 + 었다 + 어요'.

1) 멀다
far

2) 가깝다
close

3) 깔끔하다
neat, tidy

4) 삐뚤다
be crooked

5) 부드럽다
soft

6) 딱딱하다
hard

7) 편하다
comfortable

8) 불편하다
uncomfortable

9) 낫다
better

2. Create sentences using '지다/어지다/해지다' with the given words.

1) 불편하다

2) 부드럽다

3) 딱딱하다

4) 낫다

5) 가깝다

3. Complete the blanks using '지다/어지다/해지다 + ㄹ 거예요'.

1) 익숙하다
familiar, used to

2) 다르다
different

3) 같다
same

4) 밝다
bright

5) 어둡다
dark

6) 복잡하다
complicated

7) 심각하다
serious (things)

8) 따뜻하다
warm

9) 차갑다
cold (things)

4. Complete the blanks using '지다/어지다/해지다 + ㄴ 것 같다 + 아요'.

1) 희미하다
dim

2) 어색하다
awkward

3) 빠르다
fast

4) 친하다
close

5) 흔하다
common

6) 느리다
slow

7) 소홀하다
neglectful

8) 까칠하다
cynical

9) 진지하다
serious (person)

5. Create sentences using '지다/어지다/해지다' with the given words.

1) 까칠하다

2) 어색하다

3) 친하다

4) 느리다

5) 빠르다

는지
(Do you know what it is..?)

When

인지/는지

언제**인지**
shortened
to
언젠지

→ 언제**인지** 아세요?
Do you know when it is?

언제 시작하**는지** 알아요?
Do you know when it starts?

(제 생일이) 언제**인지** 아세요?
Do you know when (my birthday) is?

(공연이) 언제 시작하**는지** 알아요?
Do you know when (the show) starts?

Where

ㅆ는지/었는지/했는지 = ㄴ지/은지

어디**인지**
shortened
to
어딘지

→ 어디인지 기억나요?
Do you remember where it is?

(우리가) 어디에서 만났**는지** 기억나요?
Do you remember where we met?

(집이) 어디인지 기억나요?
Do you remember where (your house) is?

(우리가) 어디에서 만난**지** 기억나요?
I don't remember where we met.

Who

ㄹ지/을지

누구**인지**
shortened
to
누군지

→ 누군지 알아요?
Do you know who he is?

누가 올**지** 궁금해요?
Do you wonder who will come?

(이 사람이) 누구인지 알아요?
Do you know who (this person) is?

내일 누가 올**지** 몰라요.
I don't know who would come tomorrow.

What

무엇**인지**
shortened
to
뭔지

*이것이 → 이게
→ (이게) 뭔지 알아요?
Do you know what (this is)?

뭔 말인지 이해돼요?
Do you understand what I'm saying?
*무슨 → 뭔

*그것이 → 그게
(그게) 무슨 의미인지 알아요?
Do you know what (it) means?

뭘 좋아하는지 관심 없어요.
I am not interested in what you like.
*무엇을 → 뭐를 → 뭘

Why

왜**인지**
shortened
to
왠지

→ 왠지 알아요?
Do you know why?

A: (제가) 왜 외국어를 공부하는지 궁금해요?
Do you wonder why I study foreign languages?

왠지 몰라요.
I don't know why.

왜 공부하는지 알고 싶어요.
I want to know why you study them.

How

어떻다
is used
to
어떻게

→ 어떻게 하는지 알아요?
Do you know how to do it?

우리가 어떻게 만났는지 알아요?
Do you know how we met?

어떻게 하는지 몰라요.
I don't know how to do it.

어떻게 만났는지 몰라요.
I don't know how you guys met.

Note

Use ㄴ지/은지 for adjectives

Exercises Unit 17

1. Complete the blanks using '인지'. *Write both the original and the shortened form.

1) 언제   언제인지   2) 어디   3) 누구   4) 무엇   5) 왜
when   언젠지   where   who   what   why

6) 얼마   7) 노래   8) 제목   9) 소리   10) 의미
how much   song   title   sound   meaning

2. Translate the sentences using '인지' with the words above.

1) 제 생일이   ?
Do you know when my birthday is?

2) 제가   ?
Do you remember who I am?

3) 제 집이   ?
Do you want to know where my house is?

4) 저게   !
Do you know what that is?

5) 이게   ?
May I ask what this means?

6) 이게   !
Do you know what song this is?

7) 무슨   .
I don't get what it's saying.

8) 그 표가   !
Have you searched how much the ticket is on the Internet?

3. Complete the blanks using '는지'.

1) 끝나다   2) 살다   3) 만나다   4) 확인하다   5) 하다
be finished   live   meet   check   do

6) 팔다   7) 구하다   8) 기록하다   9) 보고하다   10) 말하다
sell   save, get, look for   write down   report   say

4. Translate the sentences using '는지' with the words above.

1) 수업이   ?
Do you know what time the class is finished?

2) 저는 그 남자가   .
I am not interested in where the man lives.

3) 이 제품을   알려 주세요.
Please let me know where they sell this product.

4) 제가   ?
Have you ever thought about why I like this?

5) 엄마가   .
I didn't know what my mom likes.

6) 그 여자가   .
I wonder what the woman is doing now.

5. Translate the sentences using '써는지/었는지/했는지'.

1) 제가   ?
Do you know why I came here?

2)   ?
Did you write down what you did today?

3) 그 반지를   ?
Will you let me know where you got the ring?

4) 제가   ?
Do I have to report what I did?

5) 선생님이 방금   ?
Did you hear what the teacher just said?

6) 선생님이   .
I couldn't hear what the teacher said.

6. Create conversations using '는지, 써는지, ㄹ지'.

1) A: B:

2) A: B:

3) A: B:

4) A: B:

5) A: B:

인지/ㄴ지/은지/는지
(Do you know if ...)

Nouns — 인지

초보자 → 초보자**인지** 어떻게 알아요?
beginner
How do you know if he is a beginner?

그 사람이 초보자**인지** 아닌지 어떻게 알아요?
How do you know if he is a beginner **or not**?

Adjectives — ㄴ지/은지

키가 크**다** → 그 남자가 키가 큰**지** 작은**지** 알고 싶어요.
tall
I want to know if the man is tall, or if he is short.

키가 작**다** → 그 남자가 키가 작은**지** 아니면 큰지 알고 싶어요.
short
I want to know if the man is short **or (if not)** tall.

Irregulars — ㄹ → ㄴ지, ㅂ → 운지

길다 → 긴지 짧은지 체크해 볼게요.　　　무겁다 → 무거**운지** 가벼운지 들어 볼게요.
long　　I will check If it is long (or) short.　　heavy　　I will try to lift it If it is heavy (or) light.

Verbs — 는지

되**다** → 이 선풍기가 되**는지** 확인해야 돼요.
work (things)
I have to check if this fan works.

맞**다** → 정답이 맞**는지** 물어 보세요.
correct
(Try to) Ask if the answer is correct.

Irregular — ㄹ → 는지

살**다** → 그 사람이 서울에서 사**는지** 인천에서 사는지 몰라요.
live
I don't know if the person lives in Incheon (or) Seoul.

Connection

가다 → 갈지 말지 고민중이에요.　　　　　[가다 + ㄹ지]
go
I'm thinking if I will go or not.

* 갈 것인지 → 갈 건지　　갈 것인지, 안 갈 것인지 결정하세요.　　　[가다 + ㄹ 것 + 인지]
Please decide if you are going to go or not.

갔는지 말해 주세요.　　　　　　　　　　　[가다 + ㅆ다 + 는지]
Please tell me if he left.

Exercises Unit 18

1. Answer the questions using '~인지 ~인지 모르겠어요' with the words provided.

1) A: 이 버스가 막차예요?　　B: ___________________________ (첫차 first train, 막차 last train)

2) A: 무료예요?　　B: ___________________________ (유료 not free, 무료 free)

3) A: 에어컨이에요?　　B: ___________________________ (에어컨 air conditioner, 히터 heater)

4) A: 그 말이 사실이에요?　　B: ___________________________ (사실 true, 거짓 false)

5) A: 그 소문이 진짜예요?　　B: ___________________________ (진짜 real, 가짜 fake)

2. Make sentences using '~ㄴ지 ~은지' with the words provided.

1) A: 63빌딩이 높나요?　　___________________________ (높다 high, 낮다 low)

2) A: 이 제품이 좋나요?　　___________________________ (좋다 good, 나쁘다 bad)

3) A: 놀이기구는 안전한가요?　　___________________________ (위험하다 dangerous, 안전하다 safe)

4) A: 물이 차갑나요?　　___________________________ (뜨겁다 hot, 차갑다 cold) *things

5) A: 제 목소리가 큰가요?　　___________________________ (크다 big, 작다 small)

3. Make sentences using '는지' with the words provided.

1) 정답이 맞을까요?　　___________________________ (맞다 correct, 틀리다 wrong)

2) 잘돼요?　　___________________________ (되다 work, 안 되다 doesn't work)

3) 거짓말을 하는 것 같아요.　　___________________________ (거짓말을 하다 lie, 안 하다 don't do)

4) 인터넷에서 파나요?　　___________________________ (팔다 sell, 안 팔다 don't sell)

5) 저 여자분 남자친구가 있을까요?　　___________________________ (있다 have, 없다 don't have)

4. Complete the sentences using '는지' and proper grammar.

가다	되다	어울리다	오다	좋아하다

1) A: ___________________________
I have to know if he likes me or not.
B: 그게 무슨 상관이에요. 그냥 고백하세요.

2) A: ___________________________
I didn't know if he left.
B: 진짜요? 일주일 전에 떠났어요.

3) A: ___________________________
I will ask if he came.
B: 네, 그럼 저는 여기에서 기다릴게요.

4) A: ___________________________
I want to see if this jacket suits me.
B: 피팅룸은 이쪽이니까 여기에서 갈아입으세요.

5) A: ___________________________
Can you show me if it works or not?
B: 네. 한 번 보세요. 어때요? 잘 됐죠?

ㄴ 지 얼마나 되다
(How long have you done it?)

No 받침 — ㄴ 지

오다
come
→ 온 지 얼마나 되다
how long since you came
→ 한국에 온 지 얼마나 되었어요?
How long (has it been) since you came to Korea?

A: 한국에 온 지 얼마나 됐어요?
How long (has it been) since you came to Korea?

B: 한국에 온 지 2년 됐어요.
It has been 2 years since I came to Korea.

*되었어요 is shortened to 됐어요

금연하다
quit smoking
→ 금연한 지 얼마나 되다
how long have you quit smoking
→ 금연한 지 얼마나 되었어요?
How long have you quit smoking?

A: 금연한 지 얼마나 됐어요?
How long have you quit smoking?

B: 금연한 지 1개월쯤 됐어요.
It has been about a month that I've quit smoking.

받침 — 은 지

담배를 끊다
quit smoking
→ 끊은 지 얼마나 되다
how long have you quit
→ 담배를 끊은 지 얼마나 되었어요?
How long have you quit smoking?
*한 is a sound of estimating numbers

A: 담배를 끊은 지 얼마나 됐어요?
How long have you quit smoking?

B: 담배를 끊은 지 한 1년 정도 됐어요.
It has been around a year that I quit.

치료를 받다
get treatment
→ 치료를 받은 지 얼마나 되다
How long have you gotten treatment?
→ 병원에서 치료를 받은 지 얼마나 되었어요?
How long have you gotten treatment in the hospital?

A: 병원에서 치료를 받은 지 얼마나 되었어요?
How long have you gotten treatment in the hospital?

B: 입원한 지 다섯 달 정도 됐어요.
I've been hospitalized for around 5 months.

Irregular — ㄹ → ㄴ 지 얼마나 되다

살다
live
→ 한국에서 산 지 얼마나 됐어요?
How long have you lived in Korea?

저는 한국에서 산 지 정확히 5년이 됐어요.
I have lived in Korea exactly 5 years.

Exercises Unit 19

1. Complete the blanks using '니/은 지 얼마나 됐어요?'.

1) 배우다
learn

2) 사귀다
go out (relationship)

3) 결혼하다
be married

4) 일하다
work

5) 헤어지다
break up

6) 졸업하다
graduate

7) 키우다
raise

8) 임신하다
be pregnant

9) 입원하다
be hospitalized

2. Answer the questions using '니/은 지 (　　　) 됐어요' with the time provided below, and '정도'.

1) 한국어를 공부한 지 얼마나 됐어요?

2) 여기에서 산 지 얼마나 됐어요?

3) 강아지를 키운 지 얼마나 됐어요?

4) 임신한 지 얼마나 됐어요?

5) 여행한 지 얼마나 됐어요?

| 육 개월 |
| 일주일 |
| 십 년 |
| 한 달 |
| 이틀 |

3. Make sentences using '니/은 지 (　　　) 되었다 + 고'.

1) 한국어를 배운 지 3년 되었고, 여기에서 일한 지 1년 되었어요. *되었고 → 됐고, 되었어요 → 됐어요

2)

3)

4. Make sentences using '니/은 지 (　　　) 되었다 + 는데'.

1) 한국에서 산 지 5년 정도 되었는데 아직 한국어를 못 해요. *되었는데 → 됐는데

2)

3)

5. Complete the conversations using the given words with '니/은 지 (　　　) 되었다', and '쯤'.

| 살다, 2년 | 공부하다, 1년 6개월 | 오다, 2년 |

1) A: 채영 씨, 한국어를 몇 년 동안 공부했어요? 정말 잘하시는데요? B: 저는 한국어를

2) A: 진짜요? 한국에서 오래 사셨어요? B: 네. 한국에서

3) A: 저도 한국에 　　　　　　　　　　　　　, 한국어를 잘 못해서 고민이에요.

6. Make sentences using '니/은 지 (　　　) 됐어요'.

1)

2)

3)

4)

5)

UNIT 20

ㄹ지도/을지도
(might)

                일지도 모르다

유부녀   →   유부녀일지도 몰라요.
married woman   She might be a married woman.

유부남   →   유부남일지도 몰라요.
married man   He might be a married man.

No받침/받침   ㄹ지도 모르다/을지도 모르다

쏘다   →   저 남자가 총을 쏠지도 몰라요.
shoot, sting   That man might shoot the gun.

총에 맞다   →   빈민가에 가면 총에 맞을지도 모르니까 조심하세요.
get shot   You might get shot if you go to a ghetto, so please be careful.

Irregular   ㅂ → 울지도 모르다, ㄹ → 지도 모르다

어둡다   →   어두울지도 몰라요.   힘들다   →   힘들지도 몰라요.
dark   It might be dark.   hard   It might be hard.

Connection

먹다 → 먹고 있을지도 몰라요.   [먹다 + 고 있다 + 을지도 모르다 + 아요]
eat   He might be eating.

        먹어야 될지도 몰라요.   [먹다 + 어야 되다 + ㄹ지도 모르다 + 아요]
        I might have to eat.

        할 수 있을지도 몰라요.   [하다 + ㄹ 수 있다 + 을지도 모르다 + 아요]
        I might be able to do it.

        갈지도 모르고 안 갈지도 몰라요.   [가다 + ㄹ지도 모르다 + 고, 안 + 가다 + ㄹ지도 모르다 + 아요]
        I might go, and I might not go.

        올지도 모르니까 기다려 봐요.   [오다 + ㄹ지도 + 모르다 + 니까 + 기다리다 + ㅕ 보다 + 아요]
        He might come, so let's try to wait.

        필요할지도 몰라서 가지고 왔어요.   [필요하다 + ㄹ지도 모르다 + 아서 + 가지고 오다 + 았어요]
        We might need it, so I brought it.

Exercises Unit 20

1. Complete the blanks using '일지도 몰라요'.

1) 진짜
real

2) 가짜
fake

3) 무료
free

4) 공짜
free

5) 막차
last train

6) 귀신
ghost

7) 천사
angel

8) 악마
devil

2. Complete the conversations using '일지도 몰라요' and the given words.

| 별똥별 | 진짜 | 가짜 | 공짜 | 악마 |

1) A: 이 명품가방은 진짜예요.　　　　B: 요즘 워낙에 가짜가 많아서 그 가방도

2) A: 디즈니랜드의 입장료는 너무 비싸요.　　　B: 오늘은 크리스마스라서

3) A: 우리 엄마는 천사예요.　　　　B:

3. Complete the blanks using 'ㄹ지도 몰라요/을지도 몰라요'.

1) 그렇다
so, right, yes

2) 면접을 보다
have a job interview

3) 훔쳐 가다
steal (take away)

4) 큰일 나다
be in big trouble

5) 터지다
explode

6) 이사 가다
move out

7) 들키다
be caught

8) 질투하다
be jealous

4. Complete the conversations using 'ㄹ지도 몰라요/을지도 몰라요'.

| 들키다 | 그렇다 | 면접을 보다 | 이사 가다 | 질투하다 |

1) A: 필기시험에 합격해서 곧 　　　　. 근데 정장이 없어서 큰일이에요.

2) A: 다른 남자랑 문자한 것을 들키면 남자친구가 　　　.

3) A: 내년에 하와이로 　　　.

5. Complete the sentences using 'ㄹ지도 모르다/을지도 모르다' with the proper grammar.

| 터지다 | 이사 가다 | 면접을 보다 | 훔쳐 가다 | 잡히다 |

1) A: 　　　 만지지 마세요.
It might explode, so please don't touch it.

2) A: 훔쳐 가면 　　　 큰일 날 지도 몰라요.
If you take it away, you might be caught, and you might be in big trouble.

3) A: 내일 　　　 미리 준비해야 돼요.
I might have an interview tomorrow, so I have to be ready in advance.

4) A: 벌써 　　　.
They might have taken it away already.

5) A: 다음 달에 말레이시아로 　　　.
I might have to move to Malaysia next month.

는 줄 알다
(I think you do..)

Nouns — 인 줄 알다

선생님 → 선생님인 줄 알다
teacher

깜짝이야! 선생님인 줄 알았어요.
Oh, my! I thought you were a teacher.

Adjectives — ㄴ 줄 알다 / 은 줄 알다

착하다 → 착한 줄 알다
nice

저는 그 사람이 착한 줄 알았어요.
I thought he/she was nice.

좋다 → 좋은 줄 알다
good

저는 제 자전거가 좋은 줄 알았어요.
I thought my bicycle was good.

Irregular — ㅂ → 운 줄 알다, ㄹ → 줄 알다

쉽다 → 쉬운 줄 알다
easy

쉬운 줄 알고 도전했는데 어려웠어요.
I thought it would be easy, so I went for it, but it was difficult.

Present — 는 줄 알다

자다 → 자는 줄 알다
sleep

앗, 죄송합니다. 자는 줄 알았어요.
Oops, I'm sorry. I thought you were sleeping.

죽다 → 죽는 줄 알다
die

와, 힘드네요. 죽는 줄 알았어요.
Wow, it's hard. I thought I was dying.

Past — ㄴ 줄 알다 / 은 줄 알다

가다 → 간 줄 알다
go, leave

저는 그 남자가 간 줄 알았어요.
I thought the man left.

갈아입다 → 갈아입은 줄 알다
change (clothes)

어머, 죄송해요. 이미 옷을 갈아입은 줄 알았어요.
Oops, I'm sorry. I thought you already changed your clothes.

Future/Guess — ㄹ 줄 알다 / 을 줄 알다

이기다 → 이길 줄 알다
win

이길 줄 알았어요.
I thought we would win. = I knew we would win.

있다 → 있을 줄 알다
here

여기에 있을 줄 알았어요.
I thought you were here. = I knew you were here.

1. Complete the blanks using '인 줄 알다'.

1) 칭찬
compliment

2) 행운
luck

3) 휴일
holiday

4) 공짜
free

5) 막차
last train

6) 가죽
leather

7) 제 것
mine

8) 동갑
same age

2. Make sentences using '인 줄 알다 + 았어요' with the words above .

1) 왜 반말을 해요?　　　　　　　A)

2) 오늘 왜 회사에 안 왔어요?　　　A)

3) 왜 제 책을 가지고 갔어요?　　　A)

3. Complete the blanks using 'ㄴ 줄 알다/은 줄 알다'.

1) 친하다
close (friend)

2) 가깝다
close (distance)

3) 답답하다
stuffy

4) 괜찮다
alright

5) 저렴하다
cheap

6) 지루하다
bored

7) 복잡하다
be complicated

8) 깔끔하다
neat

4. Answer the questions using 'ㄴ 줄 알다/은 줄 알다 + 았다 + 는데' with the words above .

1) 컴퓨터를 고쳐 보니까 어때요?　　A)　　　　　　　　　　생각보다 쉬웠어요.

2) 부산은 어땠어요? 재미있게 놀다가 왔어요?　A)　　　　　멀더라고요.

3) 왜 안 샀어요?　　　　　　　　A)　　　　　　　　　　가격이 너무 비싸서요.

5. Complete the blanks using 'ㄴ 줄 알다/은 줄 알다'.

1) 당첨되다
win (the lottery)

2) 뽑히다
be picked

3) 다 되다
be done

4) 끊기다
be cut off

5) 결석하다
be absent

6) 지나치다
pass (by), excessive

7) 낫다
heal, better

8) 퇴근하다
get off work

6. Answer the questions 'ㄴ 줄 알다/은 줄 알다 + 고' with the words above.

1) 왜 소리를 질렀어요?　　A) 복권에　　　　　소리를 질렀는데 당첨된 게 아니더라고요.

2) 왜 컴퓨터를 껐어요?　　A) 다운로드가　　　　껐지요.

3) 왜 택시를 타고 왔어요?　A) 막차가　　　　택시를 탔는데 아직 안 끊겼어요?

7. Make sentences using '줄 알다' with other grammar '도 되다, 면 안 되다, 야 되다, etc'.

1) 과제를 내일까지 내도 되는 줄 알고 아직 안 했어요.

2)

3)

4)

5)

UNIT 22 | 는 줄 모르다
(I don't know you do..)

인 줄 모르다

휴일 holiday	→	휴일인 줄 모르다	오늘이 휴일인 줄 몰랐어요. I didn't know today was a holiday.

Adjectives

ㄴ 줄 모르다 / 은 줄 모르다

친하다 close	→	친한 줄 모르다	그렇게 친한 줄 몰랐어요. I didn't know they were **that** close.
짧다 short	→	짧은 줄 모르다	저는 제 다리가 이렇게 짧은 줄 몰랐어요. I didn't know my legs were **this** short.

Irregular

ㅂ → 운 줄 모르다, ㄹ/ㅎ → ㄴ 줄 모르다

사납다 wild	→	사나운 줄 모르다	개가 사나운 줄 몰랐어요. I didn't know the dog was wild.

Present

는 줄 모르다

할인하다 discount	→	할인하는 줄 모르다	인터넷에서 할인하는 줄 모르고 매장에서 샀어요. I didn't know it was on sale on the Internet, so I bought it at a shop.
있다 have	→	있는 줄 모르다	여자친구가 있는 줄 몰랐어요. I didn't know he has a girlfriend.

Past

ㄴ 줄 모르다 / 은 줄 모르다

오다 come	→	온 줄 모르다	문자가 온 줄 몰랐어요. I didn't know that I got a message.
벗다 take off	→	벗은 줄 모르다	어머, 죄송해요. 옷을 벗은 줄 몰랐어요. Oops, I'm sorry. I didn't know you took off your clothes.

Future/Guess

ㄹ 줄 모르다 / 을 줄 모르다

지다 lose	→	질 줄 모르다	우리 팀이 질 줄 몰랐어요. I didn't think our team would lose.
받다 receive, get	→	받을 줄 모르다	이렇게 빨리 받을 줄 몰랐어요. I didn't think I would get it **this** fast.

Exercises Unit 22

1. Complete the blanks using '인 줄 모르다'.

1) 주인공 ___________
main character

2) 영화배우 ___________
movie actor

3) 방학 ___________
vacation

4) 직원 ___________
employee

5) 약 ___________
medicine

6) 미성년자 ___________
minor

7) 외국인 ___________
foreigner

8) 주인 ___________
owner

2. Make sentences using '인 줄 모르다 + 았어요' with the words above.

1) 왜 약을 먹었어요?   A) ___________

2) 오늘부터 방학인데 왜 학교에 나왔어요?   A) ___________

3) 사실 저는 미성년자예요.   A) ___________

3. Complete the blanks using 'ㄴ 줄 모르다/은 줄 모르다'.

1) 까다롭다 ___________
picky

2) 차갑다 ___________
cold

3) 가볍다 ___________
light

4) 대단하다 ___________
great

5) 심각하다 ___________
serious

6) 힘들다 ___________
hard

7) 무겁다 ___________
heavy

8) 민감하다 ___________
sensitive

4. Answer the questions 'ㄴ 줄 모르다/은 줄 모르다 + 았다 + 는데' with the words above.

1) A) 박스를 들어보니까 어때요? 무겁죠?   B) ___________ 생각보다 무겁네요.

2) A) 처음 일을 해 보니까 어떠세요?   B) ___________ 진짜 힘들더라고요.

3) A) 문제가 심각한가요?   B) 네. 상황이 이 정도로 ___________ 많이 심각하더라고요.

5. Complete the blanks using 'ㄴ 줄 모르다/은 줄 모르다'.

1) 보내다 ___________
send

2) 전화가 오다 ___________
get a phone call

3) 문자가 오다 ___________
get a text message

4) 그렇다 ___________
yes, be so

5) 저장하다 ___________
save, store

6) 줍다 ___________
pick up (from the floor)

7) 버리다 ___________
throw away

8) 반납하다 ___________
return

6. Answer the questions 'ㄴ 줄 모르다/은 줄 모르다 + 고' with the words above.

1) A) 왜 두 개를 보냈어요?   B) ___________ 다시 보냈네요!

2) A) 이게 뭐예요? 제가 버린 건데..   B) ___________ 주워 왔네요.

3) A) 제가 보낸 문자를 안 봤어요? 답장이 없네요.. B) ___________ 일하고 있었어요.

7. Make sentences using '줄 모르다' with other conjugations '면 안 되다, 야 되다, etc'.

1) 하면 안 되는 줄 모르고 해 버렸어요.

2) ___________

3) ___________

4) ___________

5) ___________

잖아요
(You know)

Nouns — 잖아요 / 이잖아요

저
I, me
→ A: 어떻게 했어요?
How did you do it?
B: 저잖아요. 저는 다 잘해요.
You know me. I'm good at everything.

선생님
teacher
→ A: 어떻게 이런 것들을 다 알아요?
How do you know all these things?
B: 저는 선생님이잖아요. 저는 다 알아요.
You know I am a teacher. I know everything.

Adjectives — 잖아요

유명하다
famous
→ A: 혜정 씨를 어떻게 알아요?
How do you know Ms. Hyejeong?
B: 유명하잖아요. 티비에 자주 나와요.
You know she's famous. She often comes up on TV.

많다
many, a lot
→ A: 민수 씨는 차가 두 대나 있네요?
Wow, Mr. Minsu even has two cars?
B: 돈이 많잖아요.
You know he has a lot of money.

Verbs — 잖아요

되다
work
→ A: 핸드폰이 안 되는것 같아요.
I think my phone is not working.
B: 되잖아요!
You know it works!

침을 뱉다
spit
→ A: 왜 화가 났어요?
Why did you get angry?
B: 저 사람이 침을 뱉잖아요.
You know, that person spits.

Connection

사다
buy
A: 저는 옷이 없어요.
I don't have clothes.
B: 어제 샀잖아요.　　　　[사다 + ㅆ다 + 잖아요]
You know you bought some yesterday.

듣다
listen
A: 들으세요!
Please, listen!
B: 지금 듣고 있잖아요!　　　[듣다 + 고 있다 + 잖아요]
You know I'm listening now!

하다
do
A: 왜 짜증을 내요?
Why are you annoyed?
B: 제가 다 해야 되잖아요.　[하다 + 해야 되다 + 잖아요]
You know I have to do it all.

하다
do
A: 저는 못 해요.
I can't do it.
B: 할 수 있잖아요.　　　[하다 + ㄹ 수 있다 + 잖아요]
You know you can do it.

오다
come
A: 왜 아직도 기다려요?
Why are you still waiting?
B: 올지도 모르잖아요.　[오다 + ㄹ지도 모르다 + 잖아요]
You know, he might come.

Exercises Unit 23

1. Complete the blanks using '잖아요/이잖아요'.

1) 만 원
10,000 won

2) 주인
owner

3) 손님
customer

4) 빠르다
fast

5) 느리다
slow

6) 상태가 좋다
in good condition

7) 변하다
change

8) 움직이다
move

9) 따라 하다
follow, copy

2. Answer the questions using '잖아요/이잖아요' with the given words.

1) A: 이 책은 30,000원이에요.　　B:

2) A: 제가 어떻게 알아요.　　B:

3) A: 자동차가 안 움직여요.　　B:

4) A: 왜 화가 났어요?　　B:

5) A: 왜 짜증이 났어요?　　B:

1,000원
주인
움직이다
따라 하다
인터넷이 느리다

3. Make sentences using '고 있다' with '잖아요'.

1)

2)

3)

4. Make sentences using '쓰다/었다/했다' with '잖아요'.

1)

2)

3)

5. Make sentences using '야 되다/어야 되다/해야 되다' with '잖아요'.

1)

2)

3)

6. Make sentences using '안~도 되다/안~이도 되다/안 해도 되다' with '잖아요'.

1)

2)

3)

7. Make sentences using '도 되다/어도 되다/해도 되다' with '잖아요'.

1)

2)

3)

(왜냐하면) ~거든요
(That's because ...)

Nouns
거든요 / 이거든요

*왜냐하면 → 왜냐면

동갑 → A: 둘이 존댓말을 안 쓰네요? B: (왜냐하면) 저희는 동갑이거든요.
same age Oh, the two of you don't speak in a polite way. That's because we are the same age.

군인 → A: 크리스마스인데 남자친구를 안 만나요? B: 못 만나요. 남자친구가 군인이거든요.
soldier It's Christmas, but you are not meeting your boyfriend? I can't meet him. That's because he's a soldier.

Adjectives
거든요

어리다 → A: 윤식이는 왜 그렇게 장난을 쳐요? B: (왜냐하면) 나이가 아직 어리거든요.
young Why does Yoon-sik fool around like that? That's because he is still young.

철이 없다 → A: 진환이는 왜 그렇게 엄마한테 짜증을 내요? B: (왜냐하면) 철이 없거든요.
immature Why is Jin-hwan taking it out on his mom? That's because he's immature.

Verbs
거든요

운동하다 → A: 몸이 좋네요! B: 요즘에 운동하거든요.
work out Your body is in good shape! That's because I work out these days.

살다 → A: 일본에 자주 가요? B: 네. (왜냐하면) 친한 친구가 일본에서 살거든요.
live Do you go to Japan often? Yes. That's because my close friend lives in Japan.

Connection

마시다 → A: 안 마셔요? B: 네. 저는 술을 안 마시거든요. [안 + 마시다 + 거든요]
drink You aren't drinking? Right. That's because I don't drink alcohol.

갔다 오다 → A: 오늘 왜 늦었어요? B: 병원에 갔다 왔거든요. [갔다 오다 + 았다 + 거든요]
go and back Why were you late today? That's because I went to the hospital and came back.

하다 → A: 왜 짜증을 내요? B: 제가 다 해야 되거든요. [하다 + 해야 되다 + 거든요]
do Why are you annoyed? That's because I have to do it all.

하다 → A: 숙제를 안 해요? B: 오늘까지 안 해도 되거든요. [안 해도 되다 + 거든요]
do You aren't doing your homework? That's because I don't have to do it by today.

늦다 → A: 왜 그렇게 서둘러요? B: 늦으면 안 되거든요. [늦다 + 으면 안 되다 + 거든요]
be late Why are you hurrying like that? That's because I shouldn't be late.

Exercises Unit 24

1. Complete the blanks using '거든요/이거든요'.

1) 동갑 ___________
same age

2) 대리 ___________
assistant manager

3) 과장 ___________
head of department

4) 어리다 ___________
young

5) 급하다 ___________
urgent

6) 불평하다 ___________
complain

7) 아름답다 ___________
beautiful

8) 예민하다 ___________
sensitive

9) 제작하다 ___________
manufacture

2. Complete the conversation using '거든요/이거든요'.

예민하다	미국 사람	제작하다	아름답다	저렴하다

1) A: 왜 시골에서 살고 싶어요?   B: 공기가 좋고 ___________

2) A: 서현이는 왜 그렇게 화를 잘내요?   B: 시험 때문에 ___________

3) A: 물건들이 엄청 싸네요?   B: 국내에서 저희가 직접 ___________

4) A: 왜 항상 인터넷에서 쇼핑을 해요?   B: 인터넷에서 사면 매장보다 ___________

5) A: 지희 씨는 어떻게 그렇게 영어를 잘해요?   B: 저희 아빠가 ___________

3. Make conversations using '쓰다/었다' with '거든요'.

1) A: ___________   B: ___________
2) A: ___________   B: ___________
3) A: ___________   B: ___________

4. Make conversations using '면 안 되다/으면 안 되다' with '거든요'.

1) A: ___________   B: ___________
2) A: ___________   B: ___________
3) A: ___________   B: ___________

5. Make conversations using '르 줄 알다/을 줄 알다' with '거든요'.

1) A: ___________   B: ___________
2) A: ___________   B: ___________
3) A: ___________   B: ___________

6. Make conversations using 'ㄴ 적이 있다/은 적이 있다' with '거든요'.

1) A: ___________   B: ___________
2) A: ___________   B: ___________
3) A: ___________   B: ___________

는데요?
(well, but it is?)

Nouns ····· 인데요 ·····

주인 → A: 그 차를 만지지 마세요.　　B: 제가 주인인데요?
owner　　Please don't touch the car.　　But I'm the owner? (What are you talking about?)

16일 → A: 제 친구의 생일은 8월 16일이에요.　B: 제 생일은 10일인데요?
16th　　My friend's birthday is August 16th.　Well, my birthday is on the 10th?

Adjectives ····· ㄴ데요 / 은데요 ·····

부지런하다 → A: 데릭 씨는 너무 게을러요.　　B: 저 부지런한데요?
dilligent　　Mr. Derrick is too lazy.　　But I am diligent?

많다 → A: 사람들이 많이 없네요?　　B: 많은데요?
many　　Oh, there aren't many people?　　Well, there are many? (What are you talking about?)

Verbs ····· 는데요 ·····

움직이다 → A: 세게 밀고 있어요!　　B: 안 움직이는데요?
move　　I'm pushing it hard!　　But It doesn't move?

있다 → A: 서현이는 운전을 못 해요.　　B: 저 운전 면허증이 있는데요?
have　　Seo-hyeon can't drive.　　But I have a driver's license?

Connection ·····

A: 안 해요?　　B: 하고 있는데요?　　[하다 + 고있다 + 는데요]
Don't you do it?　　Well, I'm doing it?

A: 안 했어요?　　B: 했는데요?　　[하다 + 했다 + 는데요]
You didn't do it?　　Well, I did it?

A: 안 할 거예요?　　B: 할 것인데요? *할 건데요?　[하다 + ㄹ 것이다 + 인데요]
Are you not going to do it?　　Well, I'm going to do it?

A: 안 해도 돼요.　　B: 해야 되는데요?　　[하다 + 해야 되다 + 거든요]
You don't have to do it.　　Well, I have to do it?

A: 하기 싫어요?　　B: 하고 싶은데요?　　[하다 + 고 싶다 + 은데요]
You don't want to do it?　　Well, I want to do it?

1. Complete the blanks using '인데요?'.

1) 별로	2) 제 것	3) 아직	4) 처음
not really	mine	not yet	first time

2. Complete the conversations using '인데요?', and the given words.

처음	쓰레기	제 것	별로	생신

1) A: 주인이 없으면 버릴게요.   B: _______________

2) A: 진짜 좋네요!   B: _______________

3) A: 그 게임 많이 해 봤죠?   B: _______________

3. Complete the blanks using 'ㄴ데요?/은데요?'.

1) 웃기다	2) 진지하다	3) 간단하다	4) 복잡하다
funny	serious	simple	complicated

4. Complete the conversations using 'ㄴ데요?/은데요?', and the given words.

웃기다	부지런하다	진지하다	복잡하다	간단하다

1) A: 장난치지 마세요.   B: _______________

2) A: 영화가 너무 슬프죠?   B: _______________

3) A: 어때요? 간단하죠?   B: _______________

5. Complete the blanks using '는데요?'.

1) 살아 있다	2) 떠나다	3) 움직이다	4) 밀다
alive	leave	move	push

6. Complete the conversations using '는데요?', and the given words.

움직이다	떠나다	웃기다	살아 있다	밀다

1) A: 오늘 떠나죠?   B: 내일 _______________

2) A: 안 움직이죠?   B: _______________

3) A: 죽었어요.   B: _______________

7. Complete the blanks using '는데요?' and proper grammar.

1) 가다	2) 가다	3) 가다	4) 가다
→ I go?	→ I am going?	→ I went?	→ I have to go?

8. Complete the conversations using proper grammar with '는데요?', and the given words.

끝나다	못 끝내다	움직이다	들어가다	들어오다

1) A: 아직 안 끝났죠?   B: _______________

2) A: 다 끝냈죠?   B: _______________

3) A: 오늘 집에 안 들어가도 돼죠?   B: _______________

기, 는 것
(-ing)

No받침 ---------------------------- 기 ----------------------------

*것은 → 건

배우**다** → 배우**기**는 어렵지만 굉장히 유용해요.　=　배우**는 것**은 어렵지만 굉장히 유용해요.

learn　　Learn**ing** is difficult, but it's extremely useful.　Learn**ing** is difficult, but it's extremely useful.

쓰**다** → 일기 쓰**기**는 문법을 공부할 때 도움이 돼요.　=　일기를 쓰**는 것**은 문법을 공부할 때 도움이 돼요.

use, write　Writ**ing** a diary is helpful when you study grammar.　Writ**ing** a diary is helpful when you study grammar.

받침 ---------------------------- 기 ----------------------------

돈을 벌**다** → 돈을 벌**기**는 어려운데 쓰**기**는 쉬워요.　=　돈을 버**는 것**은 어려운데 쓰**는 것**은 쉬워요.

make money　Mak**ing** money is difficult, but spend**ing** it is easy.　Mak**ing** money is difficult, but spend**ing** it is easy.

*것을 → 걸

만들**다** → 만들**기**를 좋아해요.　=　만드**는 것**을 좋아해요.

make　　I like mak**ing** it.　　I like to make it.

Note ---------------------------- Use '기' for making a list ----------------------------

My Bucket List

말하**다** → 독일어 유창하게 말하**기**　　　짓**다** → 한옥 짓**기**

speak　　Speak**ing** German fluently　　build　　Build**ing** a Hanok

담배를 끊**다** → 담배 끊**기**　　　모으**다** → 1억 모으**기**

quit smoking　Quitting smoking　　collect, save up　Saving 1 billion Won

자격증을 따**다** → 자격증 따**기**　　　쓰**다** → 자서전 쓰**기**

get a license　Getting a license　　write　　Writing an autobiography

---------------------------- 기 쉽다, 기 어렵다, 기 힘들다 ----------------------------

하**다** → 하**기** 쉽다　　　달리**다** → 달리**기** 시작하다

do　　Easy to do　　run　　start running

고치**다** → 고치**기** 어렵다　　　쓰**다** → 쓰**기** 편하다

fix　　Difficult to fix　　write, use　comfortable to use

없애**다** → 없애**기** 힘들다　　　숨쉬**다** → 숨쉬**기** 불편하다

remove　Hard to remove　　breathe　uncomfortable breathing

Exercises Unit 26

1. Complete the blanks using '기'.

1) 듣다
listen

2) 지원하다
apply

3) 합격하다
pass, be accepted

4) 다루다
handle

5) 키우다
raise

6) 설득하다
persuade

7) 설명하다
explain

8) 예측하다
predict

9) 해결하다
resolve

10) 선택하다
choose

11) 되돌리다
undo

12) 바꾸다
change

2. Translate the sentences using '기'.

1) It's hard to explain.

2) It's difficult to resolve the problem.

3) It's easy to handle.

4) It's easy to say, but hard to do.

5) It's difficult to get accepted, but I will try to apply for it.

3. Make a 'To do list' for tomorrow using '기'.

1)

2)

3)

4)

5)

4. Make a bucket list using '기'.

1)

2)

3)

4)

5)

것
(thing)

Thing — ㄴ 것/은 것

예쁘**다** → 예쁜 **것**
pretty   pretty thing

예쁜 **것**은 구하기 힘들어요.
It is hard to get something pretty.

좋**다** → 좋은 **것**
good   good thing

좋은 **것**이에요. *shortened to 좋은 거예요
It is a good thing.

Exception — ㅂ → 운 것, ㄹ → ㄴ 것, 있다/없다 → 는것

뜨겁다 → 뜨거운 **것**
hot   Hot thing

길다 → 긴 **것**
long   long thing

재미있다 → 재미있**는 것**
fun   fun thing

That I do — 는 것

바라**다** → 제가 바라**는 것**은 자동차예요.
hope   The thing that I hope is a car. = What I hope for is a car.

좋아하**다** → 제가 좋아하**는 것**은 빵이에요.
like   The thing that I like is bread. = What I like is bread.

Shortened

(것은 → 건), (것이 → 게), (것을 → 걸), (것으로 → 거로), (것이니까 → 거니까), (것이라서 → 거라서), (것인데 → 건데)

ex) (좋은 것은 → 좋은 건), (좋은 것이 → 좋은 게), (좋은 것을 → 좋은 걸), (좋은 것으로 → 좋은 거로), (좋은 것이니까 → 좋은 거니까)

ing — 는 것

*하다verbs can be nouns in 3 different ways.

말하**다** →
speak, say

말하**기**는 쉽지만 실천하**기**는 어려워요.
Speaking is easy, but acting is difficult.

*실천하다: put something into action

말하**는 것**은 쉽지만 실천하**는 것**은 어려워요.
Speaking is easy, but acting is difficult.

=

말**은** 쉽지만 실천**은** 어려워요.
Speaking is easy, but acting is difficult.

*Normal verbs can be nouns in 2 different ways.

어지르다 → 어지르**는 것**은 재미있지만 치우**는 것**은 힘들어요.
make a mess   Making a mess is fun, but tidying up is hard.

= 어지르**기**는 재미있지만 치우**기**는 힘들어요.
Making a mess is fun, but tidying up is hard.

Connection

*것이에요 shortened to 거예요

사다 → 산 것
buy   The thing that I bought

[사다 + ㄴ + 것]

산 것이에요.
It is something I bought.

사고 싶은 것
The thing that I want to buy

[사다 + 고 싶다 + 은 것]

사고 싶은 것이에요.
It is something I want to buy.

사야 되는 것
The thing that I have to buy

[사다 + 야 되다 + 는 것]

사야 되는 것이에요.
It is something I have to buy.

Exercises Unit 27

1. Complete the blanks using 'ㄴ 것/은 것'.

1) 필요하다
need

2) 크다
big

3) 소중하다
precious

4) 유용하다
useful

5) 깨끗하다
clean

6) 작다
small

7) 쓸모없다
useless

8) 차갑다
cold

2. Complete the conversations using 'ㄴ 것/은 것', and the given words.

| 작다 | 소중하다 | 쓸모없다 | 깨끗하다 | 차갑다 |

1) A: 이걸 찾고 있었어요?　　　　　　B: 너무 커요. 그것보다 　　　　　 이 필요해요.

2) A: 배가 아파요.　　　　　　B: 　　　　　 을 먹으니까 그렇지요.

3) A: 이게 뭐예요?　　　　　　B: 　　　　　 이에요. 버려 주세요.

3. Complete the blanks using '는 것'.

1) 바라다
hope

2) 비용이 들다
cost money

3) 돈을 벌다
make money

4) 걱정하다
worry

5) 바꾸다
change

6) 갖다
have

7) 인정하다
admit

8) 의심하다
doubt

4. Translate the sentences using '는 것', with correct grammar.

| 비용이 들다 | 고치다 | 쓰다 | 저렴하다 | 빠르다 | 갖다 | 괜찮다 | 바꾸다 | 위험하다 | 조심하다 |

1)
Fixing is not difficult, but it costs money.

2)
Doing it is okay, but it's dangerous, so please be careful.

3)
Spending money is easy, but making it is hard.

4)
Buying on the Internet is cheaper.

5)
Taking a bus is faster.

6)
It's something I wanted to have.

7)
It's something I changed.

8)
It's something that I can't do.

9)
It's something I am good at.

10)
Is it something I'm allowed to use?

5. Make sentences using '는 것'.

1)

2)

3)

4)

5)

보다
(than)

Nouns · 보다

버스 → 버스**보다** 기차가 **더** 빨라요. = 기차가 버스**보다** **더** 빨라요.
bus　　The train is faster than the bus.　　　The train is faster than the bus.

어제 → 어제**보다** 오늘이 **더** 추워요. = 오늘이 어제**보다** **더** 추워요.
yesterday　Today is colder than yesterday.　　Today is colder than yesterday.

하다 · 보다

생각하다 → 생각**보다** 더 오래 걸렸어요. = 생각한 것**보다** 더 오래 걸렸어요.
think　　It took longer than I thought.　　　It took longer than I thought.

일하다 → 일**보다** 건강이 **더** 중요해요. = 일하는 것**보다** 건강이 더 중요해요.
work　　Health is more important than work.　　Health is more important than work.

기 · 보다

*것이 shortened to 게

올라가다 → 올라가기**보다** 내려가기가 더 힘들어요. = 올라가는 것**보다** 내려가는 게 더 힘들어요.
go up　　Going down is more difficult than going up.　Going down is more difficult than going up.

보다 → 보기**보다** 하기가 더 어려워요. = 보는 것**보다** 하는 게 더 어려워요.
watch, see　Doing it is more difficult than watching it.　Doing it is more difficult than watching it.

는 것 · 보다

올라가다 → 올라가는 **것**보다 내려가는 것이 더 힘들어요. = 올라가**기**보다 내려가기가 더 힘들어요.
go up　　Going down is more difficult than going up.　Going down is more difficult than going up.

보다 → 보는 **것**보다 하는 것이 더 어려워요. = 보기보다 하기가 더 어려워요.
watch　　Doing it is more difficult than watching it.　Doing it is more difficult than watching it.

Exercises Unit 28

1. Complete the blanks using '보다'.

1) 외모 appearance	2) 성격 personality	3) 혈액형 blood type	4) 원숭이 monkey
5) 금 gold	6) 은 silver	7) 코끼리 elephant	8) 운 luck
9) 실력 skill	10) 시내버스 city bus	11) 고속버스 express bus	12) 통학버스 school bus

2. Create sentences using '보다' with the given words.

비싸다	중요하다	크다	보다	저렴하다

1) (시내버스, 고속버스)

2) (금, 은)

3) (외모, 성격)

4) (실력, 운)

5) (코끼리, 원숭이)

3. Complete the blanks using '는 것보다'.

1) 타다 get on, take	2) 갈아타다 transfer (to)	3) 고치다 fix	4) 주차하다 park (car)
5) 올라가다 go up	6) 내려가다 go down	7) 수술하다 have a surgery	8) 모으다 save up, collect
9) 벌다 earn, make (money)	10) 선호하다 prefer	11) 내리다 get off	12) 참다 endure

4. Create sentences using '는 것 + 보다', '는 게' with the given words.

건강에 좋다	쉽다	선호하다	낫다	어렵다

1) (엘리베이터를 타다, 걷다)

2) (운전하다, 주차하다)

3) (수술하다, 참다)

4) (돈을 벌다, 모으다)

5) (달다, 짜다)

이렇다, 그렇다, 저렇다, 어떻다
(like this, like that, how)

이렇다

이렇다 + ㄴ 것　→　이런 것은 필요없어요.　　것은 = 건
I don't need something like this.

이런 것을 왜 샀어요?　　것을 = 걸
Why did you buy something like this?

이런 것이 필요해요.　　것이 = 게
I need something like this.

이런 것으로 할 수 있어요?　것으로 = 거로
Can you do it with this?

그렇다

그렇다 + ㄴ 것　→　그런 것은 어디에서 배웠어요?　것은 =
Where did you learn something like that?

그런 것을 어떻게 알아요?　것을 =
How do you know something like that?

그런 것이 중요해요?　　것이 =
Is something like that important?

그런 것으로 못 해요.　　것으로 =
You can't do it with something like that.

저렇다

저렇다 + ㄴ 것　→　저런 것은 필요없어요.　　것은 =
I don't need something like that.

저런 것을 왜 좋아해요?　　것을 =
Why do you like something like that?

저런 것이 필요해요.　　것이 =
I need something like that.

저런 것으로요?　　것으로 =
With something like that?

어떻다

어떻다 + ㄴ 것　→　어떤 것이 필요해요?　　것이 =
Which one do you need?

어떤 것을 배우고 싶어요?　　것을 =
Which one do you want to learn?

어떤 것으로 골랐어요?　　것으로 =
Which one did you choose?

어떤 것이요? = 어떤 거요?　것 = 거
Which one?

Like this　　　　게

이렇다 + 게　→　이렇게 하세요.
like this　　　Please do it like this.

그렇게 하세요.
Please do it like that.

저렇다 + 게　→　저렇게 하세요.
like that　　　Please do it like that.

어떻게 해요?
How do I do it?

Exercises Unit 29

1. Complete the blanks using '이렇다, 그렇다, 저렇다, 어떻다 + ㄴ'.

1) 이렇다 + 곳
place like this

2) 그렇다 + 소리
sound like that

3) 저렇다 + 데
place like that

4) 이렇다 + 집
house like this

5) 그렇다 + 말
word like that

6) 저렇다 + 아이들
kids like that

7) 이렇다 + 사람
person like this

8) 그렇다 + 표정
look (face) like that

9) 저렇다 + 것
thing (stuff) like that

10) 그렇다 + 뜻
meaning like that

11) 어떻다 + 의미
which meaning

12) 어떻다 + 얘기
which story

2. Translate the sentences using '이렇다, 그렇다, 저렇다, 어떻다 + ㄴ'.

1) Do you want to live in a place like this?

2) I need something like that.

3) Don't hang out with a person like that.

4) I like stuff like this.

5) May I do it with something like this?

3. Complete the blanks using '게'.

1) 이렇다 + 게
like this

2) 그렇다 + 게
like that

3) 저렇다 + 게
like that

4. Translate the sentences using '이렇다, 그렇다, 저렇다, 어떻다 + 게'.

1) You should do it like this.

2) I want to do it like that.

3) It is hard if you do it like that.

4) Don't do it like that and, do it like this.

5) Try to do it like this.

5. Make sentences using '이렇다, 그렇다, 저렇다, 어떻다'.

1)

2)

3)

4)

5)

이, 히, 리, 기
(be done)

이

쓰다	→	쓰이다	언제 쓰여요?
use		be used	When is it used?

차다	→	차이다	여자친구한테 차였어요.
kick		be kicked	I was kicked by my girlfriend. (She broke up with me.)

히

닫다	→	닫히다	문이 닫혔어요.
close		be closed	The door is closed.

막다	→	막히다	차가 막혀서 늦었어요.
block		be blocked	My car was blocked (the traffic was heavy), so I was late.

리

물다	→	물리다	모기에 물려서 가려워요.
bite		be bitten	I was bitten by a mosquito, so it is itchy.

밀다	→	밀리다	아줌마한테 밀려서 넘어졌어요.
push		be pushed	I was pushed by a middle aged woman, so I fell.

기

잠그다	→	잠기다	문이 잠겼어요.
lock		be locked	The door was locked.

끊다	→	끊기다	와이파이가 끊겼어요.
cut off		be cut off	The wifi was cut off.

Exercises Unit 30

1. Complete the blanks using '이'.

1) 낚다   낚이다
hook

2) 쌓다
stack

3) 치다
hit

4) 베다
cut

5) 쏘다
sting

6) 쓰다
use, write

7) 섞다
mix

8) 깎다
peel

2. Create sentences using '이' and the words below.

1) 낚다

2) 쏘다

3) 쓰다

4) 치다

5) 차다

6) 베다

3. Complete the blanks using '히'.

1) 닫다
close

2) 막다
block

3) 찍다
take (a photo)

4) 뽑다
pick

5) 잡다
catch

6) 밟다
step on

7) 뒤집다
flip

8) 접다
fold

4. Create sentences using '히' and the words below.

1) 잡다

2) 뒤집다

3) 뽑다

4) 밟다

5) 막다

6) 닫다

5. Complete the blanks using '리'.

1) 흔들다
shake

2) 열다
open

3) 걸다
hang

4) 물다
bite

5) 밀다
push

6) 떨다
shake (body)

7) 자르다
cut

8) 누르다
press

6. Create sentences using '리' and the words below.

1) 흔들다

2) 열다

3) 누르다

4) 물다

5) 걸다

6) 떨다

7. Complete the blanks using '기'.

1) 숨다
hide

2) 끊다
cut off

3) 빼앗다
take away

4) 벗다
take off (clothes)

5) 잠그다
lock

6) 감다
close (eyes)

7) 남다
be left

8) 안다
hug

8. Create sentences using '기' and the words below.

1) 끊다

2) 잠그다

3) 빼앗다

4) 숨나

5) 남다

6) 안다

되다, 당하다
(be done, be done by)

하다 ┈┈┈┈┈┈┈┈┈┈┈┈┈┈┈┈┈┈┈ **되다**

*되었 → 됐

승인하다 approve	→	승인되다 be approved

회원 가입이 승인되었습니다.
The membership has been approved.

취소하다 cancel	→	취소되다 be canceled

비 때문에 콘서트가 취소됐어요.
The concert was canceled because of the rain.

완료하다 complete	→	완료되다 be completed

승인이 완료됐습니다.
The approval has been completed.

Connection ┈┈┈┈┈┈┈┈┈┈┈┈┈┈┈┈┈┈┈┈┈┈┈┈┈┈┈

취소하다 cancel	→	취소되어서 It is canceled, so	→	돼서

공연이 취소돼서 우울해요.
The show is canceled, so I'm depressed.

완료하다 complete	→	완료되었는데 It is complete, but	→	됐는데

설치가 완료됐는데 안 돼요.
The installation is complete, but it's not working.

당하다 ┈┈┈┈┈┈┈┈┈┈┈┈┈┈┈┈┈┈┈ **당하다**

배신하다 betray	→	배신당하다 be betrayed **by**

친구한테 배신당한 적이 있으세요?
Have you ever been betrayed by your friend?

퇴장하다 exit	→	퇴장당하다 be sent off **by**

유명한 축구선수가 경기장에서 퇴장당했어요.
A famous soccer player was sent off the field. (by the referee)

사기를 치다 scam	→	사기를 당하다 be scammed **by**

해외에 갔을 때 택시기사한테 사기를 당했어요.
I was scammed by a taxi driver when I went abroad.

Connection ┈┈┈┈┈┈┈┈┈┈┈┈┈┈┈┈┈┈┈┈┈┈┈┈┈┈┈

해킹하다 hack	→	해킹당해서 I was hacked by him, so

해커한테 제 계정을 해킹 당해서 아이디가 지워졌어요.
My account has been hacked by a hacker, so my ID got deleted.

무시하다 ignore	→	무시당했지만 I was ignored by them, but

사람들한테 무시당했지만 포기하지 않았어요.
I was ignored by the people, but I didn't give up.

1. Complete the blanks using '되다'.

1) 승인하다
approve

2) 정리하다
arrange

3) 파악하다
grasp

4) 설립하다
establish

5) 설치하다
install

6) 추가하다
add

7) 사용하다
use

8) 요구하다
require

9) 결제하다
pay

10) 취소하다
cancel

11) 종료하다
terminate, exit (programs)

12) 시작하다
start

2. Make sentences using '되다' + '었다' with other conjugations and the words given.

1) 추가하다

2) 시작하다

3) 요구하다

4) 완료하다

5) 설치하다

6) 결제하다

7) 취소하다

3. Complete the blanks using '당하다'.

1) 거절하다
reject

2) 무시하다
ignore

3) 설득하다
persuade

4) 배신하다
betray

5) 협박하다
threat, blackmail

6) 차별하다
discriminate

7) 이용하다
use

8) 구타하다
beat

9) 폭행하다
assault

10) 사기치다
scam

11) 해킹하다
hack

12) 도용하다
steal (name, photo, ID, email)

4. Make sentences using '당하다' with other conjugations and the words given.

1) 거절하다

2) 해킹하다

3) 설득하다

4) 무시하다

5) 사기치다

6) 구타하다

7) 배신하다

게 되다
(end up)

*게 되다 + 었다 + 어요 = 게 되었어요 shortened to 게 됐어요

No받침
게 되다

키우**다** raise	→	키우**게 되다** end up raising	오늘부터 카멜레온을 키우게 되었어요. I ended up raising a chameleon.
꿈을 이루**다** achieve the dream	→	꿈을 이루**게 되다** end up achieving a dream	드디어 제 꿈을 이루게 됐어요. I ended up achieving my dream.
참가하**다** participate	→	참가하**게 되다** end up participating	친구가 추천해서 참가하게 됐어요. My friend recommended it, so I ended up participating.

받침
게 되다

살아남**다** survive	→	살아남**게 되다** end up surviving	혼자 살아남게 되었어요. I ended up surviving alone.
알**다** know	→	알**게 되다** end up knowing	친구가 알려 줘서 알게 됐어요. My friend informed me, so I ended up knowing.
팔**다** sell	→	팔**게 되다** end up selling	요즘 잘 안 써서 팔게 됐어요. I ended up selling it because I don't use it these days.

Connection

[게 되다 + 어서 = 게 되어서 shortened to 게 돼서]

| 갈 수 있다
can go | → | 갈 수 있**게 되다**
end up being able to go | 제가 갈 수 있게 되어서 기뻐요.
I ended up being able to go, so I'm glad. |

[게 되다 + 었다 + 고 = 게 되었고 shortened to 게 됐고]

| 이민을 가다
immigrate | → | 이민을 가**게 되다**
end up immigrating | 저는 미국으로 이민을 가게 되었고 거기에서 학교를 다니게 됐어요.
I ended up immigrating to America and going to school there. |

[게 되다 + 었다 + 는데 = 게 되었는데 shortened to 게 됐는데]

| 이사를 가다
move to | → | 이사를 가**게 되다**
end up moving to | 스페인으로 이사를 가게 되었는데 뭐부터 준비해야 하나요?
I ended up moving to Spain, but what should I prepare for? |

[게 되다 + 면 = 게 되면]

| 입사하다
join a company | → | 입사하**게 되다**
end up joining a company | 그 회사에 입사하게 되면 얼마나 좋을까요?
If I end up joining the company, how good would it be? |

1. Complete the blanks using '게 되다'.

1) 퇴사하다	2) 경험하다	3) 퇴원하다
resign (quit a job)	experience	be discharged from a hospital
4) 입사하다	5) 감기에 걸리다	6) 입원하다
join a company	catch a cold	be hospitalized

2. Create sentences using '서/어서/해서' and the given words with '게 되다 + 었어요'.

> 1)(선풍기를 틀고 자다, 감기에 걸리다)   2)(넘어지다, 병원에 입원하다)   3)(돈이 없다, 아르바이트를 하다)

1)

2)

3)

3. Answer the questions using '해서' and '게 되다 + 었어요'.

1) Q. 벌써 퇴원하셨어요?   A.

2) Q. 왜 한국어를 공부해요?   A.

3) Q. 왜 입원하셨어요?   A.

4) Q. 어떻게 아세요?   A.

5) Q. 왜 퇴사하셨어요?   A.

4. Complete the blanks using '게 되다'.

1) 참여하다	2) 사귀다	3) 봉사활동하다
participate	have a relationship	do volunteer work
4) 지원하다	5) 말싸움하다	5) 이사 가다
apply	have an argument	move out

5. Create answers using '다가' and '게 되다 + 었어요'.

1) Q. 둘이 어떻게 사귀게 됐어요? A.

2) Q. 어떻게 결혼하게 됐어요?   A.

3) Q. 둘이 어떻게 알게 됐어요?   A.

4) Q. 왜 헤어졌어요?   A.

5) Q. 어떻게 우리 회사에 지원하게 됐나요? A.

6. Write a story about how you ended up studying Korean.

있다/어 있다/해 있다
(has been done)

No받침 ┈┈┈┈┈┈┈┈┈┈┈┈┈┈┈ 있다 ┈┈┈┈┈┈┈┈┈┈┈┈┈┈┈

| 서다 | → | 서 있다 | 버스 정류장에 서 있어요. |
| stand | | has been standing | He has been standing at the bus stop. |

| 켜지다 | → | 켜져 있다 | 불이 켜져 있어요. |
| be turned on | | has been on | The light has been on. |

받침 ┈┈┈┈┈┈┈┈┈┈┈┈┈ 어 있다 / 아 있다 ┈┈┈┈┈┈┈┈┈┈┈┈┈

| 앉다 | → | 앉아 있다 | 나무 위에 새가 앉아 있어요. |
| sit | | has been sitting | A bird has been sitting on the tree. |

| 젖다 | → | 젖어 있다 | 옷이 젖어 있었어요. |
| wet | | has been wet | The clothes had been wet. |

하다 ┈┈┈┈┈┈┈┈┈┈┈┈┈┈┈ 해 있다 ┈┈┈┈┈┈┈┈┈┈┈┈┈┈┈

| 위치하다 | → | 위치해 있다 | 남산타워는 서울에 위치해 있어요. |
| locate | | be located | Namsan Tower is located in Seoul. |

Irregulars ┈┈┈┈┈┈┈┈┈ Follow the present tense format ┈┈┈┈┈┈┈┈┈

| 쓰다 | → | 써 있다 | 이 책에 데릭 씨의 이름이 써 있어요. |
| write | | has been written | Derrick's name has been written in this book. |

| 갇히다 | → | 갇혀 있다 | 우리 아이가 저 안에 갇혀 있어요. |
| be stuck | | has been stuck | My child has been stuck in there. |

| 설치되다 | → | 설치되어 있다 | 모든 프로그램들이 설치되어 있어요. |
| be installed | | has been installed | All the programs have been installed. |

Connection

| 떨어지다 | → | 여기에 돈이 떨어져 있었어요. |
| be dropped | | The money had been dropped here. |

| 열리다 | → | 문이 열려 있길래 들어 왔어요. |
| be opened | | I came in because the door was open. |

Exercises Unit 33

1. Complete the blanks using '있다/어 있다/해 있다'.

1) 떨어지다 ______
be dropped

2) 버려지다 ______
be thrown away

3) 새겨지다 ______
be engraved

4) 설치되다 ______
be installed

5) 켜지다 ______
be turned on

6) 지정되다 ______
be designated

7) 등록되다 ______
be registered

8) 깔리다 ______
be buried, be installed

9) 연결되다 ______
be connected

10) 서다 ______
stand

11) 빠지다 ______
fall out

12) 매달리다 ______
hang

13) 살다 ______
live

14) 깨지다 ______
be broken (glasses)

15) 뽑히다 ______
be picked, be pulled

16) 망가지다 ______
be broken (things)

2. Complete the sentences using '어 있다/아 있다/해 있다', and the given words.

> 깔리다 등록되다 지정되다 빠지다 매달리다 새겨지다 켜지다 연결되다 떨어지다 버려지다

1) 경복궁은 문화재로 ______ 있습니다.

2) 이미 ______ 있는 아이디입니다.

3) 요즘 세상은 인터넷으로 ______ 있습니다.

4) 요즘 게임에 ______ 있어요.

5) 바닥에 천 원짜리가 ______ 있었어요.

6) 부엌에 불이 ______ 있었어요.

7) 컴퓨터에 유용한 프로그램들이 ______ 있을 거예요.

8) 바닥에 ______ 있는 쓰레기를 주웠어요.

9) 제 지갑에는 아버지의 성함이 ______ 있어요.

10) 나무에 감이 주렁주렁 ______ 있네요.

3. Complete the conversations using '있다/어 있다/해 있다', with the given words and grammar.

> 깨지다 망가지다 뽑히다 서다 설치되다

1) A: 성훈 씨를 봤어요?
B: 문 앞에 ______ [던데요]

2) A: 컴퓨터에 무슨 프로그램이 있나요?
B: 워드, 액셀, 그리고 포토샵이 ______ [습니다]

3) A: 코드를 뽑아 주세요.
B: 이미 ______ [는데요]

4) A: 누가 창문을 깼어요?
B: 저도 잘 모르겠어요. ______ [더라고요]

5) A: 왜 망가뜨렸어요?
B: 원래 ______ [었어요]

4. Make sentences using '있다/어 있다/해 있다' with other grammar.

1) ______

2) ______

3) ______

4) ______

5) ______

UNIT 34 | 게 하다, 게 만들다
(make someone do/let someone do)

No받침 · · · · · · 게 하다 · · · · · ·

슬프**다**	→	슬프**게 하다**
sad		make someone sad

여자친구가 저를 슬프게 해요.
My girlfriend makes me sad.

미치**다**	→	미치**게 하다**
crazy		drive someone crazy

아빠가 저를 미치게 해요.
My dad drives me crazy.

후회하**다**	→	후회하**게 만들다**
regret		make someone regret

후회하게 만들 거예요.
I'm going to make him regret it.

받침 · · · · · · 게 하다 · · · · · ·

스트레스를 받**다**	→	스트레스를 받**게 하다**
stress		stress someone out

친구가 스트레스를 받게 해요.
My friend stresses me out.

웃**다**	→	웃**게 하다**
laugh		make someone laugh

남편이 저를 웃게 해요.
My husband makes me laugh.

*울**다**	→	울**리다**
cry		make someone cry

누가 울렸어요?
Who made you cry?

Connection

만지**다**	→	못 만지**게 하다**
touch		don't let someone touch

아기가 위험한 물건을 못 만지게 하세요.
Please don't let the baby touch dangerous things.

운전하**다**	→	운전하**게 해 주다**
drive		let someone drive

오늘은 특별한 날이니까 제가 차를 운전하게 해 주세요.
Please let me drive the car because today is a special day.

있**다**	→	있**게 해 주다**
be somewhere		let someone be

생각할 게 많아요. 그러니까 혼자 있게 해 줄래요?
I have a lot to think about. So will you please let me be alone?

먹**다**	→	먹고 싶**게 하다**
eat		make someone want to eat

먹고 싶게 하지 마세요.
Don't make me want to eat.

성공하**다**	→	성공할 수 있**게 도와드리다**
be successful		help someone become successful

여러분이 성공할 수 있게 도와드릴게요.
I'll help you guys become successful.

자**다**	→	못 자**게 괴롭히다**
sleep		keep someone from sleeping

엄마, 형이 저를 못 자게 괴롭혀요.
Mom, older brother is bothering me and not letting me sleep.

시키다 · · · · · · (1) make someone work (2) order · · · · · ·

하다 → 시키다 (1)	A: 박스를 옮겨 주세요.	B: 저한테 시키지 마세요.
	Please move the box for me.	Do not make me do it.
시키다 (2)	A: 뭐를 시켰어요?	B: 냉면을 시켰어요.
	What did you order?	I ordered cold noodles.

Exercises Unit 34

1. Complete the blanks using '게 하다'.

1) 짜증나다
be annoyed

2) 고민하다
consider, contemplate

3) 민망하다
embarrassed

4) 놀라다
be surprised

5) 당황하다
freak out

6) 두근거리다
palpitate

2. Create sentences with the words given using '게 하다'.

1) 두근거리다

2) 민망하다

3) 놀라다

4) 당황하다

5) 고민하다

3. Complete the blanks using '게 만들다'.

1) 곤란하다
tough

2) 지치다
exhausted

3) 착각하다
be delusional, mistaken

4) 난처하다
embarrass

5) 당황하다
freak out

6) 설레다
flutter

4. Create sentences with the words given using '게 만들다'.

1) 당황하다

2) 설레다

3) 지치다

4) 난처하다

5) 착각하다

5. Complete the blanks using '시키다'.

1) 실행하다
put it into action

2) 말하다
say

3) 배달하다
deliver

4) 심부름하다
run errands (for someone)

5) 하다
do

6) 훈련하다
train

6. Create sentences with the words given using '시키다'.

1) 심부름하다

2) 배달하다

3) 훈련하다

4) 말하다

5) 실행하다

게, 히
(-ly)

No받침

빠르**다** fast, quick	→	빠르**게**
느리**다** slow	→	느리**게**
짜**다** salty	→	짜**게**

게

빠르게 움직여야 돼요.
You have to move quickly.

느리게 걸어 볼까요?
Shall we walk slowly?

음식을 너무 짜게 먹으면 몸에 안 좋아요.
It's not good for your body if you eat food too salty.

받침

짧**다** short	→	짧**게**
길**다** long	→	길**게**
재미있**다** have fun, funny	→	재미있**게**

게

머리를 짧게 자르고 싶어요.
I want to cut my hair short.

길게 만들어 주세요.
Please make it long for me.

재미있게 노세요.
Please have fun.

하다

정확하다 exact, precise	→	정확하**게**, 정확**히**
간단하다 simple	→	간단하**게**, 간단**히**
천천하다 slow	→	천천하**게**, 천천**히**

게, 히

정확히 무슨 뜻이에요?
What does that mean exactly?

간단하게 만들었어요.
I made it simple.

조금 천천히 말씀해 주시겠어요?
Would you please speak a little slowly for me?

Exercises   Unit 35

1. Complete the blanks using '게'.

1) 거칠다
   wild, rough

2) 공평하다
   fair

3) 화려하다
   fancy

4) 특별하다
   special

5) 급하다
   urgent

6) 시시하다
   boring (thing)

7) 엄격하다
   strict

8) 신중하다
   careful

9) 꼼꼼하다
   meticulous

10) 튼튼하다
    strong

11) 신속하다
    quick

12) 간단하다
    simple

2. Complete the sentences using '게'.

> 공평하다   특별하다   꼼꼼하다   엄격하다   재미있다   급하다   간단하다   시시하다   신속하다   신중하다

1) 어디를 그렇게   가세요?

2) 이곳은 출입이   제한되어 있습니다.

3) 제가   준비한 선물이에요.

4) 하자없이   작업해 주세요.

5) 학생들을 차별하지 말고   대해 주세요.

6)   노세요!

7) 지진이 났을 때는   대피하십시오.

8) 시간이 없으니까   얘기할게요.

9) 결정할 때는   결정하세요.

10) 영화가   끝났어요.

3. Complete the blanks using '히'.

1) 엄숙하다
   solemn

2) 우연하다
   coincidence

3) 완전하다
   complete

4) 조용하다
   quiet

5) 정확하다
   precise

6) 솔직하다
   honest

7) 편하다
   comfortable

8) 과감하다
   bold

9) 영원하다
   eternal

10) 자세하다
    detail

11) 분명하다
    exact, obvious

12) 꾸준하다
    steady

4. Complete the sentences using '히'.

> 완전하다   천천하다   분명하다   꾸준하다   자세하다   편하다   조용하다   영원하다   솔직하다   정확하다

1) 서두르지 말고   하세요.

2) 제가   말씀드렸잖아요.

3) 친구한테   속았어요.

4) 이 제품은   팔리고 있는 제품입니다.

6) 조금 더   설명해 주시겠어요?

6) 정답을   맞히셨습니다.

7)   쉬세요.

8)   저는 그 사람을 믿을 수 없어요.

9)   사랑힐 거예요.

10) 버스나 지하철에서는   대화하세요.

다고요
(say)

Adjectives — 다고요

나쁘다	A: 나빠요.	B: 바쁘다고요?	A: 아니요. 나쁘다고요!
bad	It's bad.	Are you saying you are busy?	No. I'm saying it is bad!
좋다	A: 좋아요.	B: 네? 춥다고요?	A: 아니요. 좋다고요.
good	It's good.	What? Are you saying it is cold?	No. I'm saying it is good.

Verbs — ㄴ다고요 / 는다고요

가다	A: 안 갈래요.	B: 간다고요?	A: 아니요. 안 간다고요.
go	I won't go.	Are you saying you are going?	No. I'm saying I'm not going.
먹다	A: 먹을게요.	B: 안 먹는다고요?	A: 아니요. 먹는다고요.
eat	I will eat.	Are you saying you don't eat?	No. I'm saying I will eat.

다고 하다

Adjectives — 다고 하다

바쁘다	바쁘다고 해요 → 바쁘대요	쉽다	쉽다고 해요 → 쉽대요
busy	Tell him that I'm busy. / He says he is busy.	easy	Tell him that It's easy. / She says it is easy.

Verbs — ㄴ다고 하다 / 는다고 하다

가다	간다고 해요 → 간대요	먹다	먹는다고 해요 → 먹는대요
go	Tell him that I'm going. / He says he is going.	eat	Tell him that I'm eating. / She says she is eating.

Connection

오다	친구가 온다고 했어요.	그만두다	*다고 얘기하다 사장님한테 그만둔다고 얘기하세요.
come	My friend said that she's coming.	quit	Tell the boss that you are quitting.
가다	제가 간다고 할 거예요.	좋아하다	*다고 듣다 선생님이 고양이를 좋아한다고 들었어요.
go	I am going to say that I'm going.	like	I heard that the teacher likes cats.
마시다	술을 마신다고 하면 안 돼요.	쉽다	*다고 생각하다 사람들은 영어가 쉽다고 생각해요.
drink	You shouldn't say that you drink alcohol.	easy	People think that English is easy.
필요없다	*다고 해서 → 대서 엄마가 필요없다고 해서 안 샀어요	가져오다	*다고 했는데 → 댔는데 언니가 카드를 가져온다고 했는데 안 가지고 왔어요.
don't need	Mom said she doesn't need it, so I didn't buy it.	bring	She said she will bring the card, but she didn't.

Note

* Shortened '대요' can only be used for 'he says, she says, they say'.
* You can change '하다' to other words like 듣다, 말하다, 얘기하다, 전하다, 믿다 etc.
* ㄴ다고 하다, 는다고 하다 are also used as 'try', but they shouldn't be shortened.
ex) 열심히 한다고 했는데 잘 안 됐어요.

Exercises Unit 36

1. Complete the blanks by asking with '다고요' and then answering with the opposite word.

1) 깊다   깊다고요?   2) 밝다   3) 얇다   4) 평범하다
deep   얕다고요!   bright   thin   ordinary

5) 얕다   6) 어둡다   7) 두껍다   8) 특별하다
shallow   dark   thick   special

2. Complete the conversations using '다고요?'.

1) A: 방이 너무 어두워요.   B:

2) A: 저는 다리가 두꺼워요.   B:

3) A: 저희 언니는 귀가 얇아요.   B:

3. Complete the conversations using the grammar that are used in sentences with '다고요?, ㄴ/는 다고요?'.

1) A: 저는 수영을 못 해요.   B: 수영을 못 한다고요?

2) A: 저는 영어를 할 수 있어요.   B:

3) A: 지금 운전하고 있어요.   B:

4) A: 지금 집에 돌아가야 돼요.   B:

5) A: 다 포기하고 싶어요.   B:

4. Complete the blanks using 'ㄴ다고 하다/는 다고 하다 + 해요'. (Use shortened way)

1) 자취하다   2) 금연하다   3) 포기하다
   live on one's own   quit smoking   give up

4) 자퇴하다   5) 가입하다   6) 탈퇴하다
leave (school)   join (a group)   leave (a group)

5. Complete the conversation using 'ㄴ다고 하다/는 다고 하다' + '해요'. (Use shortened way)

자퇴하다	가입하다	금연하다	포기하다	탈퇴하다

1) A: 서현 씨가 시험을   B: 왜요? 무슨 일이 있었어요?

2) A: 은진이가 학교를   B: 진짜요? 이유가 뭐예요?

3) A: 아빠가 오늘부터   B: 힘들걸요?

6. Complete the conversations using proper grammar with '대요'.

도 되다	는 중이다	기 싫다	면 안 되다	야 되다

1) A: 형은 수영장에 (가다)   B: 어째서 가기 싫대요?

2) A: 실내에서는 사진을 (찍다)   B: 네. 안 찍을게요.

3) A: 필요하시면 (쓰다)   B: 정말요? 감사합니다. 잘 쓸게요.

4) A: 원서를 접수하시려면 신분증을 (가지고 오다)

7. Make sentences using '다고 하다, ㄴ다고 하다 / 는다고 하다' and '해서'.

1)

2)

3)

했다고요
(said)

Adjectives/Verbs ——— 씨다고요 / 었다고요 / 했다고요 ———

기쁘**다**	A: 기뻤어요.	B: 바빴**다고요**?	A: 아니요. 기뻤**다고요**.
glad	I was glad.	Did you say you were busy?	No. I said I was glad.
먹**다**	A: 먹었어요.	B: 안 먹었**다고요**?	A: 아니요. 먹었**다고요**.
eat	I ate.	Did you say you didn't eat?	No. I said I ate.
해결하**다**	A: 제가 문제를 해결했어요.	B: 사장님이 해결**했다고요**?	A: 아니요. 제가 해결**했다고요**.
solve	I solved the problem.	Did you say your boss solved it?	No. I said I solved it.

했다고 하다

Adjectives/Verbs ——— 씨다고 하다 / 었다고 하다 / 했다고 하다 ———

떠나**다**	떠났**다고 해요** → 떠났**대요**
leave	Tell her that he left. / He says he left.
넣**다**	넣었**다고 해요** → 넣었**대요**
put in	Tell her that he put it in. / He says he put it in.
행복하**다**	행복**했다고 해요** → 행복**했대요**
happy	Tell her that you were happy. / He says she was happy.

Connection

보**다**	엄마한테 저를 봤다고 하면 안 돼요.	보**다**	*다고 말하다 엄마한테 저를 봤다고 말하면 안 돼요.
see	You shouldn't say to mom that you saw me.	see	You shouldn't tell mom that you saw me.
가**다**	아빠한테 제가 도서관에 갔다고 해 주세요.	가**다**	*다고 전하다 제가 도서관에 갔다고 전해 주세요.
go	Please tell dad that I went to the library.	go	Please tell her that I went to the library.
보**다**	이미 클럽에서 봤다고 했어요.	사**다**	*다고 얘기하다 샀다고 얘기했어요?
see	I already said that I saw you in the club.	buy	Did you say that you bought it?
보**다**	클럽에서 봤다고 하니까 엄마가 우시던데요.	팔**다**	아빠가 제 자전저를 팔았다고 하셨어요.
see	I said that I saw you in the club, so she cried.	sell	Dad said that he sold my bicycle.

Note

* Irregulars, follow the present tense format.
* Shortened 대요, 댔어요 can only be used for he, she, they.
* You can change '하다' to other words like 듣다, 말하다, 얘기하다, 전하다 etc.

Exercises Unit 37

1. Complete the blanks using '쓰다고요?/었다고요?/했다고요?'.

1) 넘어지다
fall

2) 자퇴하다
drop out

3) 잡다
catch

4) 갈아타다
transfer (bus, train, etc)

5) 해결하다
solve

6) 휴학하다
take time off (school)

7) 놓치다
miss

8) 출발하다
start

2. Complete the conversations using '쓰다고요?/었다고요?/했다고요?'

1) A: 어제 새 신발을 샀어요.　　　　　B: 어제 새 신발을 샀다고요?

2) A: 버스를 놓쳤어요.　　　　　B:

3) A: 1호선으로 갈아탔어요.　　　　　B:

4) A: 전철이 방금 막 출발했어요.　　　　　B:

5) A: 학교를 휴학하고 아르바이트를 시작했어요.　　　　　B:

3. Make conversations using '쓰다고요?/었다고요?/했다고요?'

1) A:　　　　　B:

2) A:　　　　　B:

3) A:　　　　　B:

4) A:　　　　　B:

5) A:　　　　　B:

4. Complete the blanks using '쓰다고 하다/었다고 하다/했다고 하다' + '해요'. (Use shortened way)

1) 쓰러지다
collapse

2) 실망하다
be disappointed

3) 숨다
hide

4) 떨어트리다
drop

5) 실수하다
make a mistake

6) 나가다
go out

7) 속다
be deceived

8) 헤어지다
break up

5. Complete the conversations using '쓰대요/었대요/했대요', with the words above.

1) A: 동생이 핸드폰을 바닥에　　　　　B: 진짜요? 그래서요? 고장났대요?

2) A: 형이 집에서　　　　　B: 몇 시에 나갔대요?

3) A: 오빠가 큰　　　　　B: 무슨 실수를 했대요?

4) A: 누나가 어제 길에서　　　　　B: 병원에 갔대요?

5) A: 친한 동생이 남자친구랑　　　　　B: 왜 헤어졌대요?

6. Make sentences using '쓰/었/했다고 하다'

1)

2)

3)

4)

5)

할 거라고요
(I say I'm going to~)

*ㄹ 것이다 + 라고요 = ㄹ 것이라고요 → ㄹ 거라고요

Adjectives/Verbs ──── ㄹ 거라고요 / 을 거라고요 ────

바쁘다 busy	A: 내일 바쁠 거예요. I am going to be busy tomorrow.	B: 나쁠 거라고요? Are you saying it's going to be bad?	A: 아니요. 바쁠 거라고요! No. I'm saying I am going to be busy!
작다 small	A: 라지 사이즈는 어때요? How about the large size?	B: 아마 작을걸요? It is probably small.	A: 네? 작을 거라고요? What? Are you saying it's going to be small?
갖고 가다 take	A: 제가 갖고 갈게요. I will take it.	B: 갖고 올 거라고요? Are you saying you're going to bring it?	A: 아니요. 제가 갖고 갈 거라고요. No. I'm saying I'm going to take it.

Irregulars ──── ㅂ → 울 거라고요, ㄷ → ㄹ을 거라고요, ㄹ → 거라고요 ────

춥다 cold	A: 내일 추울걸요? It is probably cold tomorrow.	B: 좋을 거라고요? Are you saying it's going to be good?	A: 아니요. 추울 거라고요! No. I'm saying it's going to be cold!

할 거라고 하다

*ㄹ 것이다 + 라고 하다 = ㄹ 것이라고 하다 → ㄹ 거라고 하다

Adjectives/Verbs ──── ㄹ 거라고 하다 / 을 거라고 하다 ────

바쁘다 busy	바쁠 거라고 해요 → 바쁠 거래요 He says he is going to be busy.	오다 come	올 거라고 해요 → 올 거래요 He says he is going to come.
좋다 good	좋을 거라고 해요 → 좋을 거래요 She says it's going to be good.	연습하다 practice	연습할 거라고 해요 → 연습할 거래요 She says she is going to practice.

Connection ────

바쁘다 busy	바쁠 거라고 했어요 → 바쁠 거랬어요 He said he is going to be busy.	보내다 send	보낼 거라고 말씀하셨어요 He said he is going to send.
좋다 good	좋을 거라고 했어요 → 좋을 거랬어요 She said it's going to be good.	돌아오다 come back	일주일 후에 돌아올 거라고 약속했어요 He promised that he's going to come back in a week.
도착하다 arrive	곧 도착할 거라고 해서 기다리고 있어요. He says he's going to arrive soon, so I am waiting.	오다 come	올 거라고 했는데 안 왔어요. He said he is going to come, but he didn't.

* 거라고 해서 → 거래서   * 거라고 했는데 → 거랬는데

Note ────

* 할 거라고 하다 can be used as 'tell' when it's not shortened. Ex) 할 거라고 하세요
* You can change '하다' to other words like 듣다, 말하다, 얘기하다, 약속하다 etc.

Exercises Unit 38

1. Complete the blanks using '을 거라고요/을 거라고요'.

1) 던지다
throw

2) 허전하다
feel empty

3) 바꾸다
change

4) 보관하다
keep

5) 갈아타다
transfer (bus, train, etc)

6) 휴학하다
take time off (school)

7) 자르다
cut

8) 관리하다
manage

2. Complete the conversations using '을 거라고요/을 거라고요?'

1) A: 내일 머리를 자를 거예요.　　　　　B:

2) A: 제가 보관할게요.　　　　　B:

3) A: 지하철을 갈아탈 거예요.　　　　　B:

4) A: 차가 오래 돼서 바꿀 생각이에요.　　　　　B:

5) A: 제가 없으면 허전할걸요?　　　　　B:

3. Complete the blanks using '을 거라고 하다/을 거라고 하다' + '해요'. (Use shortened way)

1) 복수하다
revenge

2) 글을 올리다
write on (the Internet)

3) 뽑다
elect, hire, select

4) 버리다
throw away

5) 돌아오다
come back

6) 갈아입다
change (clothes)

7) 끊다
cut off, quit

8) 추가하다
add

4. Complete the conversations using '을 거래요/을 거래요' and the words above.

1) A: 동생이 인터넷에　　　　　B: 어느 홈페이지에 올린대요?

2) A: 부모님이 내일　　　　　B: 벌써요? 다음 주에 오신다고 하지 않았어요?

3) A: 회사에서 신입 사원을　　　　　B: 몇 명을 뽑는대요?

4) A: 아빠가 담배를　　　　　B: 끊으시면 좋겠네요.

5) A: 엄마가 냉장고를　　　　　B: 버릴 거면 저한테 주세요. 제가 쓸게요.

5. Make conversations using '을 거라고요/을 거라고요' or '을 거라고 하다/을 거라고 하다'.

1) A:　　　　　B:

2) A:　　　　　B:

3) A:　　　　　B:

4) A:　　　　　B:

5) A:　　　　　B:

6. Make conversations using '을 거라고 하다/을 거라고 하다' + '해서'.

1)

2)

7. Make conversations using '을 거라고 하다/을 거라고 하다' + '했는데'.

1)

2)

냐고요
(ask)

Nouns

냐고요 / 이냐고요

전문가
expert

A: 전문가예요?
Are you an expert?

B: 제가 전문가냐고요?
Are you asking if I'm an expert?

회사원
office worker

A: 회사원이에요?
Are you an office worker?

B: 제가 회사원이냐고요?
Are you asking if I'm an office worker?

Verbs, Adjectives

냐고요

비가 내리다
rain

A: 지금 밖에 비가 내리나요?
I wonder if it's raining outside now?

B: 비가 내리냐고요?
Are you asking if it's raining?

높다
high

A: 63빌딩이 높나요?
I wonder if the 63 building is high(tall)?

B: 63빌딩이 높냐고요?
Are you asking if the 63 building is tall?

Irregular

ㄹ → 냐고요

짐을 풀다
unpack

A: 짐을 어디에 풀까요?
Where shall I unpack?

B: 짐을 어디에 푸냐고요?
Are you asking where to unpack?

냐고 하다

Verbs, Adjectives

냐고 하다 + 해요 = 냐고 해요 (내요)

힘이 세다
strong

힘이 세냐고 해요 → 힘이 세내요
He asks if I'm strong.

힘이 세냐고 했어요 → 힘이 세냈어요
He asked if I'm strong.

맞다
correct

맞냐고 해요 → 맞내요
He asks if it's correct.

맞냐고 했어요 → 맞냈어요
He asked if It's correct.

Connection

냐고 해서 → 내서, 냐고 했는데 → 냈는데

좋아하다
like

제 동료가 저한테 샌드위치를 좋아하냐고 해서 좋아한다고 했어요.
My co-worker asked me if I like sandwiches, so I said I like them.

도착하다 + 했다
get (arrive)

저희 아빠가 저한테 집에 도착했냐고 해서 도착했다고 했어요.
My dad asked me if I got home, so I said I got home.

가다 + 고 싶다
go

제 남편이 저한테 어디에 가고 싶냐고 해서 스페인에 가고 싶다고 했어요.
My husband asked where I want to go, so I said I want to go to Spain.

예약하다 + ㄹ 거다
book

제 친구가 저한테 호텔을 예약할 거냐고 물어봐서, 할 거라고 했어요.
My friend asked me if I'm going to book the hotel, so I said I did.

Ask

냐고 물어보다 + 아서 = 냐고 물어봐서

출발하다
get going

언제 출발할 거냐고 물어봐서 곧 출발한다고 했어요.
He asked when I'm going to get going, so I said I will get going soon.

Exercises Unit 39

1. Complete the blanks using '냐고요?/이냐고요?'.

1) 몇 살 ___________ 2) 무슨 요일 ___________ 3) 언제 ___________ 4) 뭐 ___________
   how old   what day   when   what

2. Answer the questions using '냐고요?/이냐고요?'.

1) A: 한국 사람이세요? B: ___________   2) A: 생일이 언제예요? B: ___________

3) A: 몇 살이세요? B: ___________   4) A: 이게 뭐예요? B: ___________

3. Complete the blanks using '냐고요?'.

1) 같다 ___________   2) 다르다 ___________   3) 틀리다 ___________   4) 맞다 ___________
   same   different   wrong   correct

4. Answer the questions using '냐고요?'.

1) A: 이거랑 이거랑 같아요? B: ___________   2) A: 이거랑 저거랑 달라요? B: ___________

3) A: 맞아요? B: ___________   4) A: 틀려요? B: ___________

5. Complete the blanks using 'ㅆ다/었다/했다' + '냐고요?'.

1) 화장하다 ___________   2) 파마하다 ___________   3) 염색하다 ___________   4) 자르다 ___________
   put on make up   get a perm   dye   cut

6. Answer the questions using 'ㅆ다/었다/했다' + '냐고요?'.

1) A: 파마했어요? B: ___________   2) A: 머리를 잘랐어요? B: ___________

3) A: 어디에서 염색했어요? B: ___________   4) A: 오늘 화장했어요? B: ___________

7. Answer the questions using the grammar that is used in sentences with '냐고요?'.

1) A: 어디에 가고 싶어요? B: ___________   2) A: 내일 출근해야 돼요? B: ___________

3) A: 뭐를 마실 거예요? B: ___________   4) A: 뭐 하고 있어요? B: ___________

5) A: 영어를 할 수 있어요? B: ___________   6) A: 여기에 와 봤어요? B: ___________

8. Make sentences using '냐고 하다' + '해서', and 'ㄴ다고 하다/는다고 하다' + '했어요'.

1) (친구가, 언제, 오다), (제가, 내일, 가다)   B: ___________

2) (남편이, 뭐를, 하고 싶다), (집에, 있고 싶다)   B: ___________

3) (후배가, 영국에, 가 봤다), (안, 가 봤다)   B: ___________

9. Make sentences using '냐고요', or '냐고 하다'.

1) ___________

2) ___________

3) ___________

라고요/으라고요
(say, tell)

Nouns

라고요/이라고요

12시
12 o'clock

A: 12시예요.
It's 12 o'clock.

B: 뭐라고요? 벌써 12시라고요?
What are you saying?
Are you saying it's already 12 o'clock?

서른 살
thirty years old

A: 스무 살이라고요?
Are you saying you are 20?

B: 아니요, 서른 살이라고요!
No, I'm saying I'm 30!

Verbs

라고요/으라고요

안경을 쓰다
wear glasses

A: 안경을 쓰세요.
Wear glasses please.

B: 네?
What?

B: 안경을 쓰라고요?
Are you telling me to wear glasses?

안경을 벗다
take off glasses

A: 안경을 벗으세요.
Take off the glasses please.

A: 안경을 벗으라고요!
I'm telling you to take off the glasses!

라고 하다/으라고 하다

Nouns

라고 하다/이라고 하다

꽃
flower

A: 꽃은 영어로 뭐라고 해요?
How do you say 꽃 in English?

B: 꽃은 영어로 플라워라고 해요.
꽃 is called flower in English.

닉
Nick

A: 안녕하세요. 저는 닉이라고 해요.
Hi, (people) call me Nick. (I'm Nick.)

B: 네, 안녕하세요. 저는 송원이라고 합니다.
Yeah, hi. I'm Song Won.

Verbs

라고 하다/으라고 하다

눈을 뜨다
open eyes

눈을 뜨라고 해요.
Tell her to open her eyes.

눈을 뜨라고 했어요.
I told her to open her eyes.

눈을 감다
close eyes

눈을 감으라고 해요.
Tell him to close his eyes.

눈을 감으라고 했어요.
I told him to close his eyes.

Connection

청소하다
clean

동생한테 청소하라고 하세요.
Tell your sister to clean it up.

바꾸다
change

색깔을 바꾸라고 전해 주세요.
Please tell her to change the color.

해결하다
solve

직접 해결하라고 할 거예요.
I'm going to tell him to solve it by himself.

고치다
fix

나쁜 습관을 고치라고 얘기할게요.
I will tell her to fix her bad habits.

가지고 가다
take

형이 가지고 가라고 해서 가지고 왔어요.
My brother told me to take it, so I brought it.
라고 해서 → 래서

버리다
throw
away

누나가 버리라고 했는데 안 버렸어요.
My sister told me to throw it away, but I didn't.
라고 했는데 → 랬는데

Note

* 라고 하다 should not be shortened to be used as 'be called'.
* You can change '하다' to other words like 명령하다, 지시하다, 얘기하다, 전하다 etc.

1. Complete the blanks using '라고요/이라고요'.

1) 몇 시 _______ 2) 막차 _______ 3) 금요일 _______ 4) 뭐 _______
  what time   the last train   Friday   what

2. Answer the questions using '라고요/이라고요' and the words above.

1) A: 오늘은 금요일이에요.   B: 오늘이 _______   2) A: 벌써 3시네요.   B: 네? _______

3) A: 이 차가 막차예요.   B: 이 차가 _______   4) A: 저는 마흔 살입니다.   B: _______

3. Complete the blanks using '라고요/으라고요'.

1) 지우다 _______ 2) 포기하다 _______ 3) 시키다 _______ 4) 치우다 _______
  erase   give up   make one work   tidy up

4. Complete the conversations using '라고요/으라고요' and the words above.

1) A: 포기하세요.   B: _______   2) A: 지우라고요?   B: 아니요, _______

3) A: 지워주시겠어요?   B: _______   4) A: 동생한테 시키세요.   B: _______

5. Complete the blanks using '라고 하다/이라고 하다' + '해요'.

1) 김밥 _______ 2) 갈비 _______ 3) 삼겹살 _______ 4) 비빔밥 _______
  Gimbap   Galbi   Samgyupsal   Bibimbap

6. Answer the questions using '라고 하다/이라고 하다' + '해요'.

1) A: 이건 뭐예요?   B: 이건 김밥 _______   2) A: 이것도 김밥이에요?   B: 아니요, 이건 갈비 _______

3) A: 저건 뭐예요?   B: 저건 삼겹살 _______   4) A: 저것도 삼겹살이에요? B: 아니요, 그건 비빔밥 _______

7. Translate the sentences using the proper grammar and '라고 하다/으라고 하다'.

1) Who told you to do it? _______   2) Do I have to tell him to do it? _______

3) Please tell him to do it. _______   4) May I tell him to do it? _______

5) I'm going to tell him to do it. _______   6) Can you tell him to do it? _______

8. Make sentences using '라고 하다' + '해서' and '써어요/었어요/했어요.

1) (엄마, 이/가, 대학교에, 가다), (가다)   B: _______

2) (아빠, 이/가, 돈을 쓰다, 지 말다), (모으다, 시작하다)   B: _______

3) (친구, 이/가, 먹어 보다), (먹어 봤다)   B: _______

9. Make sentences using '라고 하다' + '했다' + '는데' and '써어요/었어요/했어요'.

1) (동생, 이/가, 오다), (안, 가다)   B: _______

2) (천천히, 하다), (빨리, 하다)   B: _______

3) (할아버지, 사다, 지 말다), (사다)   B: _______

UNIT 41

자고요
(I say let's..)

자고요

Verbs

| 사귀**다**
have a relationship | A: 우리 사귀어요.
A: Let's have a relationship. | B: 사귀**자고요**?
A: Are you saying let's have a relationship? | A: 네. 사귀**자고요**!
A: Yes. I'm suggesting to have a relationship. |
| 말을 놓**다**
talk in a casual way | A: 우리 말을 놓지 말아요.
A: Let's not talk in a casual way. | B: 말을 놓**자고요**?
A: Are you saying let's talk in a casual way? | B: 아니요. 말을 놓지 말**자고요**.
A: No. I'm suggesting not to talk in a casual way. |

자고 하다

Verbs — 자고 하다 + 해요 = 자고 해요 (재요)

| 버리**다**
throw away | 친구가 버리**자고 해요** → 버리**재요**
Friend says let's throw it away. | 엄마가 버리**자고 했어요** → 버리**잤어요**
Mom said let's throw it away. |
| 팔**다**
sell | 동생이 팔**자고 해요** → 팔**재요**
Brother says let's sell it. | 제가 팔**자고 했어요** → 팔**잤어요**
I said let's sell it. |

Connection

떠나**다** leave	떠나**자고 하고 싶어요**. I want to say let's leave.	만들**다** make	제가 만들**자고 제안했어요**. I suggested making it.
가**다** go	그냥 가**자고 하면** 안 돼요? Shouldn't we just say let's go?	사업을 하**다** do business	같이 사업을 하**자고 제안해 볼까요**? Shall I suggest doing business together?
팔**다** sell	아빠가 팔**자고 해서** 팔았어요. Dad said let's sell it, so I sold it.	사**다** buy	엄마가 사**자고 했는데** 안 샀어요. Mom said let's buy it, but I didn't buy it.

자고 해서 → 재서   자고 했는데 → 잤는데

Note

* You can change '하다' to other words like 제안하다, 부탁하다, 빌다, 얘기하다, 말하다 etc.

Exercises Unit 41

1. Complete the blanks using '자고요'.

1) 쉬다
rest

2) 줍다
pick up

3) 훔치다
steal

4) 도망가다
run away

5) 걸다
hang

6) 버리다
throw away

7) 사귀다
have a relationship

8) 헤어지다
break up

2. Complete the conversations using '자고요?'with the words above.

1) A: 우리 헤어져요.   B:

2) A: 차를 버리고 도망갈까요?   B:

3) A: 쓰레기를 주웁시다.   B:

3. Complete the blanks using '자고 하다 + 해요'. (Use shortened way)

1) 말을 놓다
talk in a casual way

2) 포기하다
give up

3) 도전하다
challenge

4) 반말을 하다
talk in a casual way

5) 바꾸다
switch

6) 기다리다
wait

4. Complete the conversations using '자고 하다'. with the words above. (Use shortened way)

1) A: 왜 울고 있어요?   B: 남자친구가

2) A: 왜 형한테 반말을 해요?   B: 형이

3) A: 안 가요?   B: 엄마가

5. Complete the conversations using '자고 하다' + '해서' or '자고 하다' + '했는데'.

1) A: 왜 싸웠어요?   B: 친구가 싸우자고 해서 싸웠어요.

2) A: 왜 늦었어요?   B:

3) A: 왜 울어요?   B:

4) A: 왜 안 사왔어요?   B:

5) A: 왜 안 가지고 왔어요?   B:

6. Make sentences using '자고 하다' with other grammar.

1)

2)

3)

4)

5)

달라고요
(ask for, ask to)

Nouns

을/를 달라고요

돈 money	A: 시간을 주세요. Please give me time.	B: 돈을 달라고요? Are you asking for money?	A: 아니요, 시간을 달라고요. No, I'm asking for time.
표 ticket	A: 신분증을 보여 주세요. Please show me your ID.	B: 표를 달라고요? Are you asking for the ticket?	A: 아니요, 신분증을 달라고요. No, I'm asking for your ID.

달라고 하다

Nouns

달라고 하다

용돈 allowance	용돈을 달라고 할 거예요. I'm going to ask him for allowance.	기회 chance	기회를 달라고 말할 거예요. I'm going to speak to him/her and ask for a chance.
시간 time	시간을 달라고 했어요. I asked him to give me time.	선물 present	선물을 달라고 애원하지 마세요. Please do not beg and ask for a present.

Verbs

달라고 하다/어 달라고 하다/해 달라고 하다

사다 buy	조카가 장난감을 사 달라고 해요. → 사 달래요 My nephew/niece is asking to buy a toy.	애완동물을 사 달라고 했어요 → 사 달랬어요 My nephew asked to buy a pet.
열다 open	손님이 창문을 열어 달라고 해요. → 열어 달래요 A customer is asking to open the window.	손님이 열어 달라고 했어요 → 열어 달랬어요 A customer asked to open the window.
전하다 convey	이모가 이 편지를 전해 달라고 해요.→ 전해 달래요 My aunt is asking to convey this letter.	이모가 전해 달라고 했어요 → 전해 달랬어요 My aunt asked to convey this letter.

Connection

기다리다 wait	기다려 달라고 하세요. Please ask him to wait.	동생이 저한테 두부를 사 달라고 졸라서 사왔어요. My little brother pestered me for tofu, so I bought it and came.
돕다 help	도와 달라고 하는 게 어때요? Why don't you ask him for help?	도와 달라고 애원해서 도와줬어요. She begged for help, so I gave her a hand.
사다 buy	동생이 사 달라고 해서 사줬어요. My little brother asked for it, so I bought it for him.	도와 달라고 했는데 안 도와줬어요. She asked for help, but I didn't help her.

달라고 해서 → 달래서 달라고 했는데 → 달랬는데

Note

* You can change '하다' to other words like 조르다, 빌다, 애원하다, 부탁하다 etc.

Exercises Unit 42

1. Complete the blanks using '을/를 달라고요'.

1) 기회   chance

2) 여유   spare

3) 용기   courage

4) 희망   hope

5) 표   ticket

6) 자신감   confidence

7) 일   job

8) 자유   freedom

2. Complete the conversations using '달라고요?'.

1) A: 시간을 주세요.   B:

2) A: 용기를 주세요.   B:

3) A: 희망을 주세요.   B:

3. Complete the blanks using '달라고 하다 + 해요'. (Use shortened way)

1) 말을 걸다   start talking

2) 들다   lift

3) 켜다   turn on

4) 교환하다   exchange

5) 끄다   turn off

6) 틀다   turn on

4. Complete the conversations using '달라고 하다 + 했다 + 어요'.

1) A: 왜 불을 껐어요?   B: 동생이

2) A: 왜 불을 켰어요?   B: 누나가

3) A: 왜 핸드백을 들고 있어요?   B: 여자친구가

5. Complete the conversations using '달라고 하다' + '해서' or '달라고 하다' + '했는데'.

1) A: 친구랑 왜 싸웠어요?   B: 친구가 도와달라고 했는데 안 도와줘서 싸웠어요.

2) A: 왜 지각했어요?   B:

3) A: 책상을 왜 샀어요?   B:

4) A: 왜 줬어요?   B:

5) A: 오늘은 웬일로 일찍 들어왔어요?   B:

6. Make sentences using '달라고 하다' with other conjugations.

1)

2)

3)

4)

5)

UNIT 43 | 다면서요
(You said/I heard)

Nouns
라면서요/이라면서요

5시 — 5 o'clock

A: 5시예요.
It's 5 o'clock.

B: 네? 조금 아까 1시라면서요?
What? You said it was 1 o'clock a little while ago?

마흔 살 — forty years old

A: 사실 저는 마흔 살이에요.
Actually, I am forty years old.

A: 처음 만났을 때 서른 살이라면서요!
You said you were thirty when we first met!

Adjectives
다면서요

배고프다 — hungry

A: 안 먹을 거예요? 배고프다면서요?
Are you not going to eat? You said you are hungry.

B: 다이어트 중이라서 참으려고요.
I'm in the middle of a diet, so I try to be patient.

짧다 — short

A: 그 남자는 다리가 짧다면서요?
You said his legs are short?

B: 제가 언제 그랬어요?
When did I say so?

Verbs
ㄴ다면서요/는다면서요

오다 — come

A: 내일 못 갈 것 같아요.
I think I can't come tomorrow.

B: 왜요? 온다면서요.
Why? You said you are coming.

끊다 — quit (bad habits)

A: 아직도 담배를 피우세요? 끊는다면서요?
Do you still smoke? You said you will quit it?

B: 못 끊을 것 같아요. 중독된 것 같아요.
I think I can't quit. I think I'm addicted.

Irregular
ㄹ → ㄴ 다면서요

물다 — bite

조심하세요. 그 개는 물지도 몰라요.
Please be careful. The dog might bite you.

뭐라고요? 안 문다면서요.
What? You said it doesn't bite.

Connection

사다 — buy

샀다면서요?
You said you bought it?

[사다 + ㅆ다 + 다면서요]

기다리다 — wait

기다릴 거라면서요?
You said you were going to wait?

[기다리다 + ㄹ 거다 + 라면서요]

움직이다 — move

움직이지 말라면서요?
You said not to move?

[움직이다 + 지 말다 + 라면서요]

Note

다면서요 can't be used with he, she, or they.

Exercises Unit 43

Exercises   **Unit 43**

1. Complete the blanks using '라면서요/이라면서요'.

1) 봄 __________   2) 여름 __________   3) 가을 __________   4) 겨울 __________
    Spring   Summer   Fall   Winter

2. Make questions using '라면서요/이라면서요'.

1) A: 호주는 지금 __________________ ?   B: 맞아요. 여기는 지금 여름이라서 엄청 더워요.

2) A: 거기는 벌써 __________________ ?   B: 네. 봄이 와서 꽃이 많이 피었어요.

3. Complete the blanks using 'ㄴ다면서요/는다면서요'.

1) 돌아가다 __________   2) 출근하다 __________   3) 퇴근하다 __________   4) 야근하다 __________
    go back   go to work   get off work   work overtime

4. Complete the conversations using 'ㄴ다면서요/는다면서요' , and the words above.

1) A: 저는 이만 퇴근하겠습니다.   B: 벌써요? 오늘 __________________

2) A: 오늘 10시까지 근무해야 돼요.   B: 진짜요? 8시에 __________________

3) A: 저 내일 돌아가요.   B: 네? 내년에 __________________

5. Complete the blanks using '썼다/었다/했다 + 면서요'.

1) 다 하다 __________   2) 찾다 __________   3) 나가다 __________   4) 나오다 __________
    do all   find   go out   come out

6. Complete the conversations using '썼다/었다/했다 + 면서요' , and the words above.

1) A: 아직 못 끝냈어요.   B: 아직도요? __________________

2) A: 지금 나가요.   B: 아직 안 나왔어요? 1시간 전에 __________________

3) A: 아직 못 찾았어요.   B: 어제 화장실에서 __________________

7. Complete the blanks using 'ㄹ 거라면서요, 을 거라면서요'.

1) 다니다 __________   2) 그만두다 __________   3) 지원하다 __________   4) 올리다 __________
    go to (attend)   quit   apply   upload

8. Complete the conversations using 'ㄹ 거다/을 거다 + 라면서요' , and the words above.

1) A: 이 동영상은 안 올릴 거예요.   B: 유튜브에 __________________

2) A: 내일 그만둘 거예요.   B: 왜 그만두려고 해요? 계속 __________________

3) A: 마케팅 부서에 지원하려고요.   B: 인사부에 __________________

면서/으면서 (1)
(while, at the same time)

No받침	면서

보다
watch, see, look

영화를 보**면서** 팝콘을 먹고 있어요.
I'm having popcorn while I watch a movie.

런닝머신하다
run on treadmill

잘 안 들려요. 지금 런닝머신하**면서** 전화하는 것이라서요. * 것이라서요 → 거라서요
I can't hear you well. The thing is I'm on the phone while I'm on the treadmill.

받침	으면서

밥을 먹다
have a meal

밥을 먹**으면서** 핸드폰을 하면 안 돼요.
You shouldn't use your phone while you have a meal.

읽다
read

저는 책을 읽**으면서** 음악을 들으면 집중이 안 돼요.
I can't concentrate if I listen to music while I read a book.

Irregulars	ㄹ → 면서, ㄷ → ㄹ으면서

울다
cry

울**면서** 얘기했어요.
I talked while I cried.

듣다
listen

A: 음악을 들**으면서** 공부하고 싶어요.
I want to study while I listen to music.

면서/으면서 (2)
(You do it, but why can't I?)

No받침	면서

마시다
drink

대리님은 술을 마시면서 왜 저는 못 마시게 해요?
Why can't you let me drink when you drink?

하다
do

자기는 하**면서** 왜 저한테는 하지 말라고 해요?
You do it, but why do you tell me not to do it?

받침	으면서

신다
wear (shoes)

본인은 슬리퍼를 신**으면서** 왜 저는 못 신게 해요?
You wear slippers, but why do you make me not wear them?

입다
wear (clothes)

자기는 반바지를 입**으면서** 저는 못 입게 해요.
He wears shorts, but he makes me not wear them.

Connection	

공부하다
study

엄마도 어릴 때 공부를 안 했**으면서** 왜 맨날 저한테는 공부만 하라고 해요?
You didn't study either when you were young, but why do you tell me to (only) study everyday?

Exercises Unit 44

1. Complete the blanks using '면서/으면서'.

1) 박수를 치다
clap

2) 피아노를 치다
play the piano

3) 춤을 추다
dance

4) 노래를 부르다
sing a song

5) 핸드폰을 보다
look at the phone

6) 비를 맞다
get rained on

7) 게임하다
play a game

8) 거울을 보다
look into a mirror

9) 다리를 떨다
shake one's leg

2. Complete the conversations using '면서/으면서' with the given words and grammar.

1) A: 뭐 해요?   B: (노래를 듣다/공부하다)

2) A: 뭐 하고 있어요?   B: (박수를 치다/노래를 부르다)

3) A: 뭐 하고 싶어요?   B: (게임하다/라면을 먹다)

4) A: 뭐 할 거예요?   B: (드라마를 보다/쉬다)

5) A: 어떻게 하다가 사고가 났대요? B: (핸드폰을 보다/횡단보도를 건너다)

3. Complete the conversations using '면서/으면서' with the given words and grammar.

1) A: 아빠는 맨날 티비를 (   ) 왜 저는 못 보게 하세요?

2) A: 저 사람한테는 아무말도 안 (   ) 왜 저한테만 뭐라고 하세요?

3) A: 선생님도 담배를 (   ) 왜 저한테는 피우지 말라고 하세요?

4) A: 자기도 안 했(   ) 왜 남한테 하라고 하세요?

5) A: 할 수 있(   ) 왜 못 한다고 했어요?

4. Make sentences using '면서/으면서'.

1)

2)

3)

4)

5)

다가
(Something happened while I was doing)

*다가 shortened to 다

No받침 — 다가

자르다	→	자르다가
cut		while cutting

종이를 자르다가 손가락을 베었어요.
While cutting the paper I cut my finger.

요리하다	→	요리하다가
cook		while cooking

요리하다가 다쳤어요.
While cooking I got hurt.

고민하다	→	고민하다가
ponder		while pondering

고민하다가 빨간 차를 사기로 결정했어요.
While pondering I decided to buy a red car.

받침 — 다가

졸다	→	졸다가
nod off		while nodding off

버스에서 졸다가 못 내렸어요.
While nodding off on the bus I couldn't get off.

읽다	→	읽다가
read		while reading

책을 읽다가 갑자기 아이디어가 떠올랐어요.
While reading a book, an idea came up all of a sudden.

한눈을 팔다	→	한눈을 팔다가
look away		while looking away

한눈을 팔다가 넘어졌어요.
While looking away I fell down.

Past — 다가

먹다	→	먹었다가
eat		while I ate

먹었다가 뱉었어요.
While eating I spit it up.

예약하다	→	예약했다가
book		while I booked

Z 호텔을 예약했다가 마음이 바뀌어서 취소했어요.
While booking Z hotel I changed my mind, so I canceled it.

투자하다	→	투자했다가
invest		while I invested

주식에 투자했다가 돈을 다 잃었어요.
While investing on stocks I lost all my money.

Exercises Unit 45

1. Complete the blanks using '다가'.

1) 까불다
fool around

2) 장난치다
fool around

3) 치우다
put away

4) 욕심을 부리다
be greedy

5) 지나가다
pass by

6) 피하다
avoid

7) 비교하다
compare

8) 고민하다
ponder, contemplate

9) 사업하다
do business

10) 따라 하다
copy (imitate)

11) 지나가다
pass by

12) 한눈을 팔다
look away

2. Answer the questions using the words given, and '다가', '써어요/었어요/했어요'.

1) A: 뭐 하다가 다쳤어요?   B: (핸드폰, 보다, 면서, 걷다, 넘어지다)

2) A: 무슨 상처예요?   B: (계단, 뛰다, 다치다)

3) A: 왜 지각했어요?   B: (버스, 졸다, 못, 내리다)

4) A: 어떻게 발견했어요?   B: (방, 청소하다, 발견하다)

5) A: 회사에 다니세요?   B: (회사, 다니다, 그만두다)

3. Answer the questions using the words given, and '다가'.

1) A: 왜 혼났어요?   B:

2) A: 왜 늦었어요?   B:

3) A: 왜 다쳤어요?   B:

4) A: 왜 넘어졌어요?   B:

5) A: 왜 싸웠어요?   B:

4. Write sentences using '다가'.

1)

2)

3)

4)

5)

느라고
(from/because of + negative)

*느라고 shortened to 느라

No받침   느라

돌보다 look after	→	돌보느라 from looking after

아기를 돌보느라 정신이 없어요.
It's hectic because I'm taking care of my baby.

쓰다 write	→	쓰느라 from writing

책을 쓰느라 눈이 나빠졌어요.
My eyesight got bad from writing books.

구경하다 look around	→	구경하느라 from looking around

퍼레이드를 구경하느라 시간가는 줄 몰랐어요.
I didn't know the time was going by because I was watching the parade.

받침   느라

잡다 catch	→	잡느라 from catching

모기를 잡느라 한숨도 못 잤어요.
I couldn't sleep at all because I was catching a mosquito.

듣다 listen	→	듣느라 from listening

음악을 듣느라 잘 못들었어요.
I couldn't hear well because I was listening to music.

닦다 wipe	→	닦느라 from wiping

3시간동안 접시를 닦느라 점심도 못 먹었어요.
I didn't even have lunch because I was washing the dishes for three hours.

Irregulars   ㄹ → 느라

만들다 make	→	만드느라 from making

샌드위치를 만드느라 늦었어요.
I'm late from making the sandwiches.

벌다 make (money)	→	버느라 from making money

돈을 버느라 결혼도 못 했어요.
I couldn't get married because I was making money.

먹고살다 eat and live	→	먹고사느라 from eating and living

먹고사느라 바쁘게 지내요.
I have been busy with daily life (eating and living).

Exercises Unit 46

1. Complete the blanks using '느라'.

1) 작업하다 ____
work

2) 챙기다 ____
pack, take, take care

3) 돌보다 ____
look after

4) 집중하다 ____
concentrate

5) 샤워하다 ____
take a shower

6) 도와주다 ____
lend a hand

7) 준비하다 ____
get ready

8) 얘기하다 ____
talk

9) 생각하다 ____
think

10) 밤을 새우다 ____
stay up all night

11) 내다 ____
pay

12) 시험을 보다 ____
take an exam

2. Answer the questions using the words given and '느라'.

1) A: 요즘 어떻게 지내세요?   B: (아기를 돌보다, 정신이 없다, 어요)

2) A: 뭐 하느라 늦게 주무셨어요?   B: (이것 저것 생각하다, 늦게 자다, ㅆ어요)

3) A: 친구한테 부탁해 보세요.   B: (일하다, 바쁘다, ㄹ걸요)

4) A: 왜 전화를 안 받았어요?   B: (샤워하다, 모르다, 았어요)

5) A: 뭐 하느라 밤을 새웠어요?   B: (시험공부하다, 밤을 새우다, 었어요)

3. Answer the questions using '느라' and 'ㅆ어요/었어요/했어요'.

1) A: 왜 숙제를 안 했어요?   B:

2) A: 왜 지각했어요?   B:

3) A: 왜 답장을 안 해요?   B:

4) A: 왜 아직 결혼을 안 했어요?   B:

5) A: 왜 돈이 없어요?   B:

4. Write sentences using '느라'.

1)

2)

3)

4)

5)

<table>
<tr><td>UNIT 47</td><td><h1>ㄹ 만하다/을 만하다</h1> (not bad, worth, deserve) </td></tr>
</table>

No 받침   ㄹ 만하다

| 쓰다 | → | 쓸 만하다 | 이 카메라는 조금 오래되었지만 (그럼에도 불구하고) 쓸 만해요. |
| use | | worth using | This camera is a bit old, (nevertheless) it's worth using it. |

| 타다 | → | 탈 만하다 | 이 차는 나온 지 꽤 되었는데도 아직 탈 만해요. |
| ride | | okay to ride | It's been quite a while since this car came out, but it's okay to ride. |

| 1등하다 | → | 1등할 만하다 | 이번 시합은 우리 팀이 1등할 만해요. |
| win first place | | deserve to win first place | Our team deserves to win first place in this match. |

받침   을 만하다

| 받다 | → | 받을 만하다 | 이번에는(이번엔) 창민이가 상을 받을 만해요. |
| receive | | deserve to receive | Chang-Min deserves the award this time. |

| 입다 | → | 입을 만하다 | 옷 사이즈가 딱 맞지는 않지만 입을 만해요. |
| wear | | okay to wear | The size is not a 100% fit, but it's okay to wear it. |

| 앉다 | → | 앉을 만하다 | 의자가 조금 딱딱하긴 하지만 앉을 만해요. |
| sit | | okay to sit | The chair is a little hard, but it's worth sitting on. |

Connection   It means 'worth' if you use it with 보다/어 보다/해 보다 grammar

| 하다 | → | 해 보다 | 그렇게 안 어려워요. 한 번쯤은 해 볼 만해요. |
| do | | try | It's not that difficult. It's worth trying once. |

| 가다 | → | 가 보다 | 페루는 죽기 전에 가 볼 만한 여행지 중의 한 곳이에요. |
| go | | try to go | Peru is one of the travel spots that is worth going to before you die. |

| 마시다 | | 마셔 보다 | 조금 쓰긴 하지만 마셔 볼 만해요. |
| drink | | try to drink | It is a little bitter, but worth drinking. |

Exercises Unit 47

1. Complete the blanks using '울 만하다/을 만하다'.

1) 욕먹다 __________
be blamed

2) 칭찬하다 __________
compliment

3) 불평하다 __________
complain

4) 견디다 __________
put up with

5) 참다 __________
endure

6) 대결하다 __________
fight

7) 질투하다 __________
jealous

8) 고민하다 __________
ponder

9) 자랑하다 __________
show off

10) 적응하다 __________
adapt

11) 지내다 __________
spend (time)

12) 버티다 __________
hold up

2. Complete the conversations using '울 만하다/을 만하다 + 해요' with the given words.

불평하다	보다	견디다	욕을 먹다	지내다

1) A: 손님들은 불평이 많아요.　　B: __________ . 직원들도 불친절하고 음식도 맛이 없잖아요.

2) A: 대리님이 사람들한테 욕을 먹었어요.　　B: __________ . 맨날 지각하잖아요.

3) A: 군대에서 하는 훈련은 어때요?　　B: 힘들긴 한데 __________

4) A: 그 영화가 무섭다고 들었어요.　　B: 무섭긴 한데 __________

5) A: 새 직장은 어때요? 잘 적응했어요?　　B: __________

3. Complete the conversations using '보다/어 보다/해 보다 + 울 만하다/을 만하다 + 해요' with the given words.

가다	다니다	타다	도전하다	대결하다

1) A: 경주는 어때요? 너무 멀지 않아요?　　B: 두, 세 시간 정도 걸리는데 한 번쯤은 __________

2) A: 스카이다이빙을 해 봤어요? 어때요?　　B: __________

3) A: 요즘 요가 학원에 다니죠? 어때요?　　B: __________

4) A: 롤러코스터를 타는 것이 무섭지 않나요?　　B: __________

5) A: 상대 팀은 작년에 우승한 팀이에요.　　B: __________

4. Write sentences using '울 만하다/을 만하다'.

1) __________

2) __________

3) __________

4) __________

5) __________

기는 하다
(It's true that it is ..., indeed)

*기는 shortened to 긴

No 받침 · · · · · · · · · · · · · · · 긴 하다 · · · · · · · · · · ·

슬프**다** → 슬프**긴 하다** = 슬프**긴** 슬프**다**
sad · · · · · · · · It is true that it is sad

그 영화가 슬프긴 해요.
The movie is sad, indeed.

복잡하**다** → 복잡하**긴 하다** = 복잡하**긴** 복잡하**다**
complicated · · · Indeed, it's complicated

조금 복잡하긴 한데 할 수 있을 것 같아요.
It is true that it is a little complicated, but I think I can do it.

= 조금 복잡하긴 복잡한데 할 수 있을 것 같아요.

받침 · · · · · · · · · · · · · · · · · 긴 하다 · · · · · · · · · · ·

맵**다** → 맵**긴 하다** = 맵**긴** 맵**다**
spicy · · · · · · · Indeed, it's spicy

맵긴 한데 먹을 만해요.
It is indeed spicy, but it's okay to eat.

작**다** → 작**긴 하다** = 작**긴** 작**다**
small · · · · · · · Indeed, it's small

조금 작긴 한데 쓸 수 있을걸요?
It is true that it's a little small, but we can probably use it?

= 조금 작긴 작은데 쓸 수 있을걸요?

Verbs · · · · · · · · · · · · · · · · 긴 하다 · · · · · · · · · · ·

기타를 치**다** → 치**긴 하다** = 치**긴** 치**다**
play the guitar · · It is true that I play

기타를 치긴 하는데 잘 못쳐요.
It is true that I play the guitar, but I am not good at it.

먹**다** → 먹**긴 하다** = 먹**긴** 먹**다**
eat · · · · · · · · It is true that I eat

저는 생선을 먹긴 하는데 좋아하지는 않아요.
It is ture that I eat fish, but I don't like it.

= 저는 생선을 먹긴 먹는데 좋아하지는 않아요.

Connection ·

공부하다 → 공부를 하긴 했는데 자신이 없어요.
study · · · · · It is true that I studied, but I'm not confident.
[긴 하다 + 했다 + 는데]

운동하다 → 운동을 하고 싶긴 한데 시간이 없어요.
work out · · · It is true that I want to work out, but I don't have time.
[고 싶다 + 긴 하다 + ㄴ데]

Exercises   Unit 48

1. Complete the blanks using both '긴 하다' and the each words.

1) 멀다   멀긴 하다   2) 맵다 ___________   3) 짜다 ___________   4) 궁금하다 ___________
far   멀긴 멀다   spicy   salty   wonder

5) 고맙다 ___________   6) 작다 ___________   7) 느리다 ___________   8) 부담스럽다 ___________
thank   small   slow   feel uncomfortable

2. Answer the questions using the words that are used in the questions with '긴 하다 + ㄴ데'.

1) A: 안 매워요?   B: ___________________ 먹을 만해요.

2) A: 사이즈는 안 작아요?   B: ___________________ 입을 만해요.

3) A: 그 컴퓨터는 속도가 느리지 않아요?   B: ___________________ 쓸 만해요.

4) A: 스노우보드는 위험하지 않아요?   B: ___________________ 해 볼 만해요.

5) A: 수술할 때 아프지 않아요?   B: ___________________ 참을 만해요.

3. Complete the sentences using '긴 하다 + ㄴ데'.

| 있다 | 고맙다 | 어렵다 | 느리다 | 위험하다 |

1) 노트북이 옛날 거라서 조금 ___________ 아직 쓸 수 있어요.

2) 패러글라이딩은 ___________ 죽기 전에 꼭 한 번 해 보고 싶어요.

3) 선물을 받아서 ___________ 조금 부담스러워요.

4) 중국어는 한자 때문에 ___________ 매일 연습하면 잘할 수 있어요.

5) 돈이 ___________ 부족해요.

4. Complete the sentences using '긴 하다', and the grammar that is used in questions with 'ㄴ데/는데'.

| 먹다 | 숙제를 하다 | 보다 | 치다 | 혼나다 |

1) A: 어제 집에 늦게 들어갔는데 안 혼났어요?   B: ___________________ 많이 안 혼났어요.

2) A: 또 드세요? 점심밥을 안 드셨어요?   B: ___________________ 조금밖에 안 먹었어요.

3) A: 오늘 숙제를 해야 된다고 하지 않았어요?   B: ___________________ 하기 싫어요.

4) A: 기타를 칠 줄 알아요?   B: ___________________ 잘 못쳐요.

5) A: 이 사람을 본 적이 있어요?   B: ___________________ 기억이 잘 안 나요.

5. Write sentences using '긴 하다 + ㄴ데/는데'.

1) ____

2) ____

3) ____

길래
(so + past)

No받침   길래

예쁘다 pretty	→	예쁘길래 it was pretty, so

지나가다가 예쁘길래 하나 샀어요.
I was passing by and it was pretty, so I bought it.

물어 보다 ask	→	물어 보길래 (somebody) asked, so

외국인이 길을 물어보길래 알려줬어요.
A foreigner asked me the way, so I let him know.

욕을 하다 swear, curse	→	욕을 하길래 (somebody) cursed, so

아저씨가 갑자기 저한테 욕을 하길래 저도 했어요.
A man suddenly cursed at me, so I did it to him.

받침   길래

작다 small	→	작길래 it was small, so

스몰사이즈가 조금 작길래 교환했어요.
Small size was a little small, so I exchanged it.

마음에 들다 like	→	마음에 들길래 I liked it, so

마음에 들길래 하나 샀어요.
I bought one because I liked it.

없다 don't have, there isn't	→	없길래 there was nothing, so

아무도 없길래 그냥 왔어요.
I just came because nobody was there.

Connection

바쁘다 busy	→	바쁜 것 같길래 인사도 못 하고 그냥 나왔어요. I couldn't say hello because he seemed busy.	[바쁘다 + ㄴ 것 같다 + 길래]
비슷하다 similar	→	비슷해 보이길래 몇 개 구매했어요. It looked similar, so I bought some.	[비슷하다 + 해 보이다 + 길래]
먹다 eat	→	여자친구가 젤리를 먹고 싶어하길래 사줬어요. My girlfriend wanted to eat a jelly, so I bought it for her.	[먹다 + 고 싶다 + 어하다 + 길래]

Note

길래 has the meaning of 'so' which we studied, but 서/어서/해서 are not able to
conjugate into the past tense. However 길래 can, and you can't use 길래 with '제가, 저는'.

Exercises Unit 49

1. Complete the blanks using '길래'.

1) 쳐다보다 stare	2) 놀리다 tease, make fun of	3) 무시하다 ignore	4) 할인하다 discount
5) 따라오다 follow	6) 소리를 지르다 shout	7) 물어보다 ask	8) 알려주다 inform
9) 열이 나다 have a fever	10) 기침이 나다 cough	11) 충동구매하다 impulse buy	12) 갔다 오다 go and comeback

2. Complete the sentences using '길래'.

> 놀리다　　　따라오다　　　없다　　　물어보다　　　있다

1) A: 오빠랑 왜 싸웠어요?　　　B: 오빠가 제 친구를 ＿＿＿＿＿ 화가 나서 싸웠어요.

2) A: 왜 경찰에 신고를 했어요?　　　B: 모르는 사람이 계속 저를 ＿＿＿＿＿ 무서워서 경찰에 신고했어요.

3) A: 학생한테 왜 정답을 알려줬어요?　　　B: 학생이 정답을 ＿＿＿＿＿ 그냥 알려줬어요.

4) A: 왜 남의 물건을 가지고 왔어요?　　　B: 책상 위에 ＿＿＿＿＿ 가지고 왔어요.

5) A: 왜 벌써 왔어요?　　　B: 아무도 ＿＿＿＿＿ 그냥 왔어요.

3. Complete the sentences choosing the right grammar points.

1) (열이 나다, 고, 기침이 나다, 길래, 병원에, 갔다 오다, 았다, 어요)

＿＿＿＿＿＿＿＿＿＿＿＿＿＿＿＿＿＿＿＿＿＿＿＿＿

2) (백화점에서, 50%, 을/를, 할인하다, 길래, 충동구매하다, ㅆ다/었다/했다, 어요)

＿＿＿＿＿＿＿＿＿＿＿＿＿＿＿＿＿＿＿＿＿＿＿＿＿

3) (형, 이/가, 같이, 가다, 자고 하다, 길래, 따라가다, ㅆ다/었다/했다, 어요)

＿＿＿＿＿＿＿＿＿＿＿＿＿＿＿＿＿＿＿＿＿＿＿＿＿

4) (멋지다, ㄴ/은, 차, 이/가, 지나가다, 길래, 부럽다, 서/어서/해서/워서, 계속, 쳐다보다, 었다/았다, 어요)

＿＿＿＿＿＿＿＿＿＿＿＿＿＿＿＿＿＿＿＿＿＿＿＿＿

5) (동생, 이/가, 저, 을/를, 무시하다, 길래, 소리를 지르다, 었다/았다, 어요)

＿＿＿＿＿＿＿＿＿＿＿＿＿＿＿＿＿＿＿＿＿＿＿＿＿

4. Write sentences using '길래'.

1) ＿＿＿＿＿＿＿＿＿＿＿＿＿＿＿＿＿＿＿＿＿＿＿＿＿

2) ＿＿＿＿＿＿＿＿＿＿＿＿＿＿＿＿＿＿＿＿＿＿＿＿＿

3) ＿＿＿＿＿＿＿＿＿＿＿＿＿＿＿＿＿＿＿＿＿＿＿＿＿

4) ＿＿＿＿＿＿＿＿＿＿＿＿＿＿＿＿＿＿＿＿＿＿＿＿＿

5) ＿＿＿＿＿＿＿＿＿＿＿＿＿＿＿＿＿＿＿＿＿＿＿＿＿

하다/어하다/해하다
(He/she is being ...)

No받침

하다

| 예쁘다 | → | 예뻐하다 | 할머니는 손자만 예뻐하세요. |
| pretty | | | My grandmother only has eyes for her grandson. |

| 기쁘다 | → | 기뻐하다 | 여러분, 기뻐해 주세요. |
| glad | | | Guys, please be happy for me. |

받침

어하다/아하다

| 힘들다 | → | 힘들어하다 | 저희 어머니가 요즘 힘들어하세요. |
| hard | | | My mother is having a hard time these days. |

| 좋다 | → | 좋아하다 | 저희 아버지가 좋아하세요. |
| good | | | My father likes it. |

하다

해하다

| 피곤하다 | → | 피곤해하다 | 동생이 피곤해해요 |
| tired | | | My brother is tired. |

| 심심하다 | → | 심심해하다 | 조카가 심심해해서 놀아 줬어요. |
| bored | | | My nephew was bored, so I played with him. |

Irregulars

Follow the present tense format

| 부럽다 | → | 부러워하다 | 주위 사람들이 부러워해요. |
| envy | | | People around me envy me. |

| 무섭다 | → | 무서워하다 | 여러분, 무서워하지 마세요. |
| be scared | | | Guys, don't be afraid. |

Connection

| 보다 | → | 여자친구가 영화를 보고 싶어 해요. | [보다 + 고 싶다 + 어 하다 + 해요] |
| watch | | My girlfriend wants to see a movie. | |

| 외롭다 | → | 동료가 외로워해서 제 친구를 소개시켜줬어요. | [외롭다 + 워하다 + 해서] |
| lonely | | My colleague was lonely, so I introduced my friend to her. | |

Exercises Unit 50

1. Complete the blanks using '하다/어하다/해하다'.

1) 슬프다 sad	2) 외롭다 lonely	3) 불안하다 anxious	4) 궁금하다 wonder
5) 그립다 miss	6) 부담스럽다 feel uncomfortable	7) 창피하다 embarrassed	8) 쑥스럽다 shy

2. Complete the sentences using '하다/어하다/해하다 + 해요'.

1) 제 동창은 학창시절을 ________ (그립다)
2) 오빠가 제 선물을 ________ (부담스럽다)
3) 제 아들이 ________ (불안하다)
4) 제 동생이 ________ (궁금하다)
5) 제 친구가 ________ (외롭다)
6) 제 딸이 ________ (슬프다)

3. Complete the sentences using the given words and grammar.

1) 언니가 ________ 위로해 줬어요. (슬프다, 어하다, 해서)
2) 할머니가 ________ 알려줬어요. (궁금하다, 해하다, 시다, 어서)
3) 우리 아이가 ________ (창피하다, 해하다, 는 것 같다, 아요)
4) 그 사람도 저를 ________ (그립다, 워하다, ㄹ 지도 모르다, 아요)
5) 삼촌이 ________ 아무 말도 하지 마세요. (슬프다, 어하다, 시다, ㄹ 테다, 니까)

4. Complete the blanks using '고 싶다 + 어 하다'.

1) 따라 하다 copy (imitate)	2) 키우다 raise	3) 바꾸다 change	4) 알리다 inform
5) 복수하다 revenge	6) 빌리다 borrow	7) 배우다 learn	8) 갖다 have

5. Complete the sentences using '고 싶다 + 어하다 + 해요' or '하세요'.

1) 우리 아이는 미술을 ________ (배우다)
2) 제 남편은 차를 ________ (바꾸다)
3) 제 아내는 목걸이를 ________ (갖다)
4) 저희 누나는 고양이를 ________ (키우다)
5) 기자들은 소식을 ________ (알리다)
6) 사람들은 부자가 ________ (되다)
7) 강아지가 햄을 ________ (먹다)
8) 삼촌은 시골로 ________ (내려가다)
9) 이모는 해외로 ________ (이민가다)
10) 제 동창이 일을 ________ (그만두다)

6. Write sentences using '고 싶다 + 어하다 + 해요'.

1) ________

2) ________

3) ________

UNIT 51 | ㄹ 때마다/을 때마다
(everytime I do)

| 지치다 | → | 저는 지칠 때마다 여행을 떠나요. |
| exhausted | | I go on a journey everytime I'm exhausted. |

| 심심하다 | → | 저는 심심할 때마다 친구랑 수다를 떨어요. |
| bored | | I chat with my friend everytime I'm bored. |

| 지나가다 | → | 이곳을 지나갈 때마다 옛날 생각이 나요. |
| pass | | I think of the old days everytime I pass this place. |

| 카드를 찍다 | → | 카드를 찍을 때마다 소리가 나요. |
| swipe a card | | It makes a sound everytime I swipe the card. |

| 머리를 감다 | → | 머리를 감을 때마다 머리카락이 빠져요. |
| wash hair | | My hair falls out everytime I wash my hair. |

| 이를 닦다 | → | 이를 닦을 때마다 피가 나요. |
| brush one's teeth | | I bleed everytime I brush my teeth. |

| 힘들다 | → | 여기는 제가 힘들 때마다 오는 곳이에요. |
| hard | | This is the place where I come everytime I have a hard time. |

| 코를 풀다 | → | 저는 코를 풀 때마다 코피가 나요. |
| blow one's nose | | I have a nosebleed everytime I blow my nose. |

| 지겹다 | → | 저는 일이 지겨울 때마다 게임을 해요. |
| sick and tired | | I play a game everytime I'm sick and tired of working. |

Exercises Unit 51

1. Complete the blanks using 'ㄹ 때마다/을 때마다'.

1) 숨을 쉬다
breathe

2) 제안하다
suggest

3) 바람이 불다
wind blow

4) 어지럽다
dizzy

5) 하품하다
yawn

6) 추가하다
add

7) 환승하다
transfer

8) 상담하다
consult

9) 거절당하다
get refused

10) 카드를 찍다
swipe a card

11) 헷갈리다
get confused

12) 괴롭다
painful

2. Complete the conversations using 'ㄹ 때마다/을 때마다', and the given words.

1) 제안하다   거절을 당해서 기분이 안 좋아요.

2) 어지럽다   약을 드세요.

3) 환승하다   카드를 찍어야 돼요.

4) 오다   헷갈려서 길을 잃어요.

5) 바람이 불다   꽃잎이 떨어져요.

3. Make sentences using 'ㄹ 때마다/을 때마다', and the given words.

1) (거절당하다, 기분이 나쁘다)

2) (추가하다, 돈을 내다)

3) (생각하다, 괴롭다)

4) (숨을 쉬다, 냄새가 나다)

5) (하품하다, 눈물이 나다)

4. Write sentences using 'ㄹ 때마다/을 때마다'.

1)

2)

3)

4)

5)

ㄹ 때까지/을 때까지
(until)

Noun ----------------------------------- 까지 -----------------------------------

새벽 1시 1 a.m.	→	저는 어제 새벽 1시까지 작업했어요. I worked until 1 a.m. yesterday.

No받침 ----------------------------------- ㄹ 때까지 -----------------------------------

지나가다 pass (by)	→	차가 지나갈 때까지 기다려야 돼요. You should wait until the car passes.
해가 뜨다 the sun rises	→	친구랑 해가 뜰 때까지 춤을 연습했어요. I practiced dancing with my friend until the sun rose.
합격하다 pass (exam)	→	시험에 합격할 때까지 포기하지 않을 거예요. I am not going to give up until I pass the exam.

받침 ----------------------------------- 을 때까지 -----------------------------------

죽다 die	→	죽을 때까지 잊지 않을게요. I will not forget until I die.
익다 be cooked (ripen)	→	생선이 익을 때까지 참으세요. Please be patient until the fish is cooked.
받다 receive	→	전화를 받을 때까지 할 거예요. I am going to do it until she receives (answers) the call.

Irregulars ----------------------------------- ㄹ → 때까지, ㅂ → 울 때까지 -----------------------------------

바람이 불다 wind blows	→	바람이 불 때까지 기다려 볼까요? Shall we try to wait until the wind blows?

Connection -----------------------------------

[하다 + ㄹ 수 있다 + 을 때까지]

하다 do	→	할 수 있을 때까지 계속해서 도전할 거예요. I'm going to keep challenging myself until I can do it.

[사 주다 + ㄴ다고 하다 + ㄹ 때까지]

조르다 pester	→	아빠가 차를 사 준다고 할 때까지 조를 거예요. I'm going to pester Dad until he says he will buy me a car.

Exercises   Unit 52

1. Complete the blanks using '-ㄹ 때까지/-을 때까지'.

1) 터지다
   burst

2) 달성하다
   achieve

3) 만족하다
   be satisfied

4) 이해하다
   understand

5) 해가 뜨다
   the sun rises

6) 해가 지다
   the sun sets

7) 되다
   work (function)

8) 마음에 들다
   like

9) 합격하다
   pass (exam)

10) 죽다
   die

11) 답장하다
   reply

12) 나오다
   come out

2. Make sentences using '-ㄹ 때까지/-을 때까지' and the given words.

1) (되다, 하다)

2) (이해하다, 설명하다)

3) (해가 지다, 도서관에 있다)

4) (목표를 달성하다, 노력하다)

5) (마음에 들다, 다시 하다)

3. Make sentences using '-ㄹ 때까지/-을 때까지' and the given words.

1) 배가 터지다

2) 죽다

3) 답장하다

4) 나오다

5) 만족하다

4. Make sentences using '-ㄹ 때까지/-을 때까지'.

1)

2)

3)

4)

5)

ㄹ 리가 없다/을 리가 없다
(There is no way that ..., It can't be)

Nouns ┄┄┄┄┄┄┄┄ 일 리가 없다 ┄┄┄┄┄┄┄┄

사장님
boss
→ 사장님일 리가 없다 → 그 사람이 사장님일 리가 없어요.
There's no way that he/she is the boss.

변호사
lawyer
→ 변호사일 리가 없다 → 그 남자가 변호사일 리가 없어요.
There's no way that he/she is a lawyer.

No받침 ┄┄┄┄┄┄┄┄ ㄹ 리가 없다 ┄┄┄┄┄┄┄┄

틀리다
wrong
→ 이 비밀번호가 틀릴 리가 없어요.
There's no way that this password is wrong.

기억하다
remember
→ 엄마가 그 사건을 기억할 리가 없어요.
There's no way that my mom remembers the case.

받침 ┄┄┄┄┄┄┄┄ 을 리가 없다 ┄┄┄┄┄┄┄┄

먹다
eat
→ 채식주의자들이 고기를 먹을리가 없어요.
There's no way that vegetarians eat meat.

맞다
correct
→ 이 답이 맞을리가 없어요.
There's no way that this answer is correct.

Irregulars ┄┄┄┄┄ ㄹ → 리가 없다, ㅎ → ㄹ 리가 없다 ㅂ → 울 리가 없다 ┄┄┄┄┄

알다
know
→ 사람들이 저에 대해서 알 리가 없어요.
There's no way that people know about me.

그렇다
yes, no, right
→ 그럴 리가 없어요.
It can't be true.

Connection ┄┄┄┄┄┄┄┄┄┄┄┄┄┄┄┄┄┄┄┄┄┄┄┄┄┄┄┄┄┄┄┄┄┄┄

[끝내다 + ㅆ다 + 을 리가 없다 + 어요]

끝내다
finish
→ 숙제를 벌써 끝냈을 리가 없어요.
There's no way that he finished his homework already.

[일하다 + 고 싶다 + 어 하다 + ㄹ 리가 없다 + 어요]

일하다
work
→ 사람들이 매일 일하고 싶어할 리가 없어요.
There's no way that people want to work everyday.

Exercises Unit 53

1. Complete the blanks using '='리가 없다/을 리가 없다'.

1) 거짓말 ....
lie

2) 진짜 ....
real

3) 스님 ....
monk

4) 사실 ....
true

5) 가볍다 ....
light

6) 무겁다 ....
heavy

7) 뜨겁다 ....
hot

8) 차갑다 ....
cold

9) 지다 ....
lose

10) 알다 ....
know

11) 모르다 ....
don't know

12) 그렇다 ....
yes, right

2. Complete the conversations using 'ㄹ 리가 없다/을 리가 없다 + 어요', and the given words.

진짜	거짓말	싫어하다	12시	눈이 내리다

1) A: .... B: 어떻게 확신해요?

2) A: .... B: 믿기 어렵겠지만 진짜예요.

3) A: 개는 고양이를 싫어해요. B: 개가 고양이를 ....

4) A: 12시예요. B: 벌써 ....

5) A: 밖에 눈이 와요. B: 지금 ....

3. Complete the conversations using 'ㄹ 리가 없다/을 리가 없다 + 어요', with the given words & grammar.

하다	오다	해 보다	지다	떠나다

1) A: 그 남자는 어제 떠났어요. B: 확실해요? 그 사람이 ....

2) A: 우리 팀이 지고 있어요. B: 우리 팀이 ....

3) A: 제 남편은 저한테 거짓말을 해 본 적이 없어요. B: 그분이 거짓말을 ....

4) A: 지선 씨는 중국어를 할 수 있어요. B: 그 분이 중국어를 ....

5) A: 선생님이 오셨어요. B: 선생님이 여기까지 ....

4. Write sentences using 'ㄹ 리가 없다/을 리가 없다 + 어요'.

1) ....

2) ....

3) ....

4) ....

5) ....

ㄹ 수밖에 없다/을 수밖에 없다
(I have no choice but to, I will have to)

Nouns — 밖에 없다

이것	→	이것밖에 없다	→	이것밖에 없어요.
this				I only have this.

만 원	→	만 원밖에 없다	→	주머니에 만 원밖에 없어요.
10,000 won				I only have 10,000 won in my pocket.

No받침 — ㄹ 수밖에 없다

부르다	→	계속 이렇게 행동하면 부모님을 부를 수밖에 없어요.
call (someone)		If you keep acting like this, I have no choice but to call your parents.

신고하다	→	계속 저를 협박하시면 경찰에 신고할 수밖에 없어요.
report		If you keep threatening me, I will have to report it to the police.

받침 — 을 수밖에 없다

뺏다	→	우리가 이기려면 깃발을 뺏을 수밖에 없어요.
take (from someone)		We will have to take the flag if you are trying to win.

끊다	→	건강해지기 위해서는 술과 담배를 끊을 수밖에 없어요.
cut off, quit		You will have to quit smoking and drinking alcohol to be healthy.

Irregulars — ㄹ → 수밖에 없다 / ㅂ → 울 수밖에 없다 / ㅅ → 을 수밖에 없다

갈다	→	이 부품은 너무 오래 돼서 갈 수밖에 없어요.
change		This part is too old, so you have no choice but to change it.

짓다	→	요즘 집이 너무 비싸서 스스로 지을 수밖에 없어요.
build		Houses are too expensive these days, so I have no choice but to build it myself .

Connection

[도망가다 + ㄹ 수밖에 없다 + 었다 + 어요]

도망가다	도망갈 수밖에 없었어요.
run away	I didn't have any choice but to run away. (I had to run away.)

[의심하다 + ㄹ 수밖에 없다 + 지 않다 + 아요]

의심하다	의심할 수밖에 없지 않아요?
doubt	Won't I have to doubt it?

Note

ㄹ/을 수밖에 없다 + 었다 can be used as 'had to'

Exercises Unit 54

1. Complete the blanks using 'ㄹ 수밖에 없다/을 수밖에 없다'.

1) 진행하다
proceed

2) 신고하다
report

3) 가입하다
join

4) 압수하다
seize

5) 틀다
turn on

6) 지우다
erase

7) 탈퇴하다
leave (a group)

8) 그만두다
quit

9) 끊다
cut off

10) 책임지다
take responsibility

11) 돌아가다
go back

12) 추방하다
deport

2. Complete the sentences using 'ㄹ 수밖에 없다/을 수밖에 없다 + 어요' and the given words.

책임지다	돌아가다	가입하다	틀다	압수하다

1) A: 날씨가 너무 더워서 에어컨을

2) A: 인터넷에서 옷을 사려면 회원으로

3) A: 버스터미널에 10시까지 도착하려면 지금

4) A: 제가 시작한 것이니까 제가

5) A: 수업시간에 핸드폰을 계속 사용하면

3. Complete the conversations using 'ㄹ 수밖에 없다/을 수밖에 없다 + 었어요' and the given words.

그만두다	신고하다	끊다	틀다	탈퇴하다

1) A: 왜 전화를 끊었어요?　　　　　　　　B: 주위에 사람들이 있어서

2) A: 왜 회사를 그만뒀어요?　　　　　　　B: 과장님 때문에

3) A: 왜 그룹에서 탈퇴하셨어요?　　　　　B: 문제가 생겨서

4) A: 왜 119에 신고하셨어요?　　　　　　B: 불이 나서

5) A: 왜 히터를 트셨어요?　　　　　　　　B: 날씨가 추워서

4. Make sentences using 'ㄹ 수밖에 없다/을 수밖에 없다'.

1)

2)

3)

4)

5)

버리다/어 버리다/해 버리다
(Just do it)

No받침 — — — — — — — — — — — — 버리다 — — — — — — — — — — — —

떠나다 leave	→	떠나 버리다 just leave	답답하면 떠나 버리세요. Just leave if you feel frustrated.
사다 buy	→	사 버리다 just buy	기분이 좋아서 다 사 버렸어요. My feeling was good, so I just bought it all.

받침 — — — — — — — — — — 어 버리다 / 아 버리다 — — — — — — — — — —

숨다 hide	→	숨어 버리다 just hide	자꾸 귀찮게 하면 숨어 버릴 거예요. If you keep bothering me, I will just hide.
녹다 melt	→	녹아 버리다 just melt	아이스크림이 10초만에 녹아 버렸어요. The ice cream just melted in 10 seconds.

하다 — — — — — — — — — — — — 해 버리다 — — — — — — — — — — — —

말하다 say, tell	→	말해 버리다 just say	친구한테 저의 비밀을 다 말해 버렸어요. I just told my friend all my secrets.
무시하다 ignore	→	무시해 버리다 just ignore	이상한 사람들은 무시해 버리세요. Please, just ignore strange people.

Irregulars — — — — — — — Follow the present tense format — — — — — — —

지우다 erase	→	지워 버리다 just erase it	필요없는 줄 알고 지워 버렸어요. I thought it was unnecessary, so I just erased it.
자르다 cut	→	잘라 버리다 just cut	머리가 너무 길어서 짧게 잘라 버리고 싶어요. My hair is too long, so I just want to cut it short.
보다 see	→	봐 버리다 just see	보면 안 되는 것을 봐 버렸어요. I just saw a thing that I shouldn't see.

Exercises Unit 55

1. Complete the blanks using '버리다/어 버리다/해 버리다'.

1) 던지다	2) 자르다	3) 밀다	4) 그만두다
throw	cut	push	quit

5) 녹다	6) 차단하다	7) 도망가다	8) 놓치다
melt	block	run away	miss

9) 끊다	10) 지우다	11) 삭제하다	12) 멈추다
hang up, cut off	erase	delete	stop

2. Complete the conversations using '버리다 + 었어요', and the given words.

자르다	밀다	놓치다	던지다	도망가다

1) A: 왜 머리를 잘랐어요?　　　　　　B: 너무 길어서

2) A: 왜 공을 던졌어요?　　　　　　　B: 너무 화가 나서

3) A: 왜 도망갔어요?　　　　　　　　B: 너무 놀라서

4) A: 왜 놓쳤어요?　　　　　　　　　B: 너무 미끄러워서

5) A: 왜 밀었어요?　　　　　　　　　B: 너무 화나게 해서

3. Complete the sentences choosing the right grammar points.

1) (직장, 을/를, 그만두다, 버리다/어 버리다/해 버리다, 고 싶다, 어요)

2) (사진, 을/를, 삭제하다, 버리다/어 버리다/해 버리다, ㄹ 거예요/을 거예요)

3) (이상하다, ㄴ/은, 사람, 은/는, 차단하다, 버리다/어 버리다/해 버리다, 세요/으세요)

4) (그냥, 가다, 버리다/어 버리다/해 버리다, 면/으면, 어떻게 하다, 해요)

5) (전화, 을/를, 끊다, 버리다/어 버리다/해 버리다, 는 게 어때요)

4. Write sentences using '버리다/어 버리다/해 버리다'.

1)

2)

3)

4)

5)

놓다/어 놓다/해 놓다
= 두다 / 어 두다 / 해 두다
(leave, do and put it on.., in advance)

No받침 ---- 놓다 ----

| 빼**다** | → | 빼**놓다** | 저만 빼 놓고 어디에 갔다 왔어요? |
| take out | | leave out | Where have you been without me? |

| 켜**다** | → | 켜**놓다** | 화장실 불을 켜 놓고 왔어요. |
| turn on | | leave the light on | I left the light on in the bathroom, and came. |

받침 ---- 어 놓다 / 아 놓다 ----

*놓았어요 shortened to 놨어요

| 넣**다** | → | 넣**어 놓다** | 지갑을 서랍에 넣어 **놓았어요**. |
| put in | | put in, and keep | I put my wallet in the drawer. |

| 열**다** | → | 열**어 놓다** | 창문을 열어 놓고 와서 돌아가야 돼요. |
| open | | leave it open | I left the door open, so I have to go back. |

하다 ---- 해 놓다 ----

| 설거지**하다** | → | 설거지**해 놓다** | 설거지를 다 해 놓고 나가야 돼요. |
| do the dishes | | finish the dishes | I have to finish the dishes and go out. |

| 얘기**하다** | → | 얘기**해 놓다** | 집주인한테 얘기해 **놓았으니까** 그냥 가면 돼요. |
| talk | | talk in advance | I have talked to the landlord, so you can just go. |

*놓았으니까 shortened to 놨으니까

Connection

넣다	→	[어 놓다 + 을 테다 + 니까]
		과일을 냉장고에 넣어 놓을 테니까 꺼내 드세요.
put in		I will put and keep the fruit in the fridge, so take it out and eat it.

예약하다	→	[해 놓다 + 았다 + 으니까]
		미리 방을 예약해 놓았으니까 가서 쓰시면 돼요.
book		I booked a room in advance, so you can go and use it.

빨래를 걷다	→	[어 놓다 + 으세요]
		지금 비가 내리니까 빨래를 걷어 놓으세요.
bring in the laundry		It's raining now, so please bring in the laundry.

Note ---- Follow the present tense format ----

Exercises Unit 56

1. Complete the blanks using '놓다/어 놓다/해 놓다'.

1) 넣다 put in	2) 빼다 take out	3) 남기다 leave	4) 널다 hang the laundry
5) 켜다 turn on	6) 끄다 turn off	7) 보관하다 store, keep	8) 정리하다 tidy up
9) 맡기다 leave it to someone	10) 치우다 put away	11) 빨래하다 do the laundry	12) 막다 block

2. Complete the conversations using '놓다/어 놓다/해 놓다 + 았다 + 어요' and the given words.

열다	켜다	정리하다	맡기다	넣다

1) A: 빵은 어디에 있어요?　　　　　B: 전자레인지에

2) A: 에어컨을 켜 주세요.　　　　　B: 이미

3) A: 가방은 어디에 있어요?　　　　B: 친구한테

4) A: 창문이 열려 있네요?　　　　　B: 제가

5) A: 방이 깨끗하네요.　　　　　　B: 엄마가

3. Complete the sentences using '놓다/어 놓다/해 놓다' + '았다' + '으니까' and the given words.

다 하다	틀다	다운로드하다	맡기다	넣다

1)　냉장고에 만두를　　　　　꺼내서 드세요.

2)　작업을　　　　　확인 해 보세요.

3)　옷을 세탁소에　　　　　들어올 때 갖다 주세요.

4)　보일러를　　　　　곧 따뜻해질 거예요.

5)　영화를　　　　　시간이 있을 때 보세요.

4. Make sentences using '놓다/어 놓다/해 놓다'.

1)

2)

3)

4)

5)

가다/어 가다/해 가다
(go, on its way, almost)

No받침 ——————————— 가다 —————————

| 끝나**다** | → | 끝나 **가다** | 영화가 거의 끝나 가요. |
| be finished | | | The movie is almost finished. |

| 훔치**다** | → | 훔쳐 **가다** | 누군가가 제 지갑을 훔쳐 갔어요. |
| steal | | | Someone has stolen my wallet. |

받침 ——————————— 어 가다 / 아 가다 —————————

| 죽**다** | → | 죽**어** 가다 | 선인장이 죽어 가요. |
| die | | | My cactus is dying. |

| 날**다** | → | 날**아** 가다 | 새가 반대쪽으로 날아 간 것 같아. |
| fly | | | I think the bird flew away to the opposite side. |

하다 ——————————— 해 가다 —————————

| 변**하다** | → | 변**해** 가다 | 많은 것들이 빠르게 변해 가고 있어요. |
| change | | | Many things are changing fast. |

| 환전**하다** | → | 환전**해** 가다 | 미국에 가기 전에 은행에 들러서 달러로 환전해 가야 돼요. |
| exchange money | | | I have to stop by the bank and exchange it for dollars before I go to America. |

Connection ———————————————————————

| 싸다 | → | 싸 **가다** | 병원에 음식을 싸 가도 되나요? |
| pack | | | I wonder if I can I bring food to the hospital? |

| 완료되다 | → | 완료되**어** 가다 | 설치가 완료되어 가는 중이에요. |
| be completed | | | The installation is in the middle of being completed. |

| 사라지다 | → | 사라져 **가다** | 동물이 사라져 가고 있어요. |
| disappear | | | Animals are disappearing. |

Note ———————— Follow the present tense format ————————

1. Complete the blanks using '가다/어 가다/해 가다'.

1) 뛰다 run	2) 알다 know	3) 되다 work	4) 완성되다 be completed
5) 챙기다 take, pack, take care	6) 끝나다 be finished	7) 훔치다 steal	8) 죽다 die
9) 지나다 pass by, go by	10) 사다 buy	11) 마무리하다 finish working	12) 돌다 turn

2. Complete the conversations using '가다/어 가다/해 가다' with the given words and grammar.

잘되다	완성되다	알다	쓰다	챙기다

1) A: 제품은 완성되었나요?   B: 아직이요. 근데 거의 _______________ (고 있어요)

2) A: 그 남자랑 무슨 사이예요?   B: 남자친구는 아니고, _______________ (는 중이에요)

3) A: 일은 _______________ ? (요/어요/해요) B: 네. 열심히 하고 있어요. 아마 다음 주쯤이면 끝날 것 같아요.

4) A: 책을 다 썼어요?   B: 꾸준히 _______________ 아직 못 끝냈어요. (고 있다 + 긴 하다 + ㄴ데)

5) A: 여행갈 때 수건을 _______________ (세요/으세요) B: 호텔에 수건이 없어요?

3. Complete the sentences choosing the right grammar points.

1) (거의, 다 하다, 가다/어 가다/해 가다, 니까/으니까, 조금, 만, 기다리다, 주세요/어 주세요/해 주세요)

____

2) (음식, 이/가, 거의, 다 되다, 가다/어 가다/해 가다, 니까/으니까, 식탁에, 앉다, 세요/으세요)

____

3) (밤에, 춥다, 울지도 모르다, 니까/으니까, 옷, 을/를, 넉넉히, 챙기다, 가다/어 가다/해 가다, 세요/으세요)

____

4) (새, 이/가, 날다, 가다/어 가다/아 가다/해 가다, ㅆ어요/었어요/했어요)

____

5) (위험하다, 니끼/으니까, 뛰다, 가다/어 가다/해 가다, 지 말다, 고, 천천히, 가다, 세요/으세요)

____

4. Write sentences using '가다/어 가다/해 가다'.

1) _______________

2) _______________

3) _______________

4) _______________

5) _______________

오다/어 오다/해 오다
(come, have come)

No받침 — 오다

기다리**다**	→	기다려 오다	이 순간이 오기만을 기다려 왔어요.
wait		have been waiting	I've been waiting for this moment to come.
싸**다**	→	싸 오다	제가 도시락을 싸왔어요.
pack		pack and come	I packed a lunch box and came.

받침 — 어 오다 / 아 오다

찍**다**	→	찍어 오다	외국에서 사진을 많이 찍어 왔어요.
take a picture		take a picture and come	I took a lot of photos and came from abroad.
날**다**	→	날아 오다	저쪽에서 공이 날아 왔어요.
fly		fly in	The ball flew in from over there.

하다 — 해 오다

준비**하다**	→	준비해 오다	이 대회에 참가하기 위해 2년동안 준비해 왔어요
prepare		have been preparing	I've been preparing for this competition for 2 years.
훈련**하다**	→	훈련해 오다	지진 대피를 위한 훈련을 해 왔어요.
train		have been training	I have been training to avoid earthquakes.

Connection

연구하다	→	10년이 넘게 사진을 찍어 오고 연구해 왔지만 아직도 잘 모르겠어요.
study, research		I've been taking pictures and studying them for over 10 years, but I still don't get it.
지켜보다	→	그 사람은 제가 오랫동안 지켜봐 와서 잘 알아요.
keep one's eyes on		I know the person well because I've been keeping my eyes on him for a long time.

Note

Follow the present tense format

Exercises Unit 58

1. Complete the blanks using '오다/어 오다/해 오다'.

1) 챙기다 __________
take, pack

2) 연구하다 __________
research

3) 뛰다 __________
run

4) 걷다 __________
walk

5) 찾다 __________
find, look for

6) 참가하다 __________
participate

7) 싸다 __________
pack

8) 키우다 __________
raise

9) 사다 __________
buy

10) 날다 __________
fly

11) 돌다 __________
turn

12) 생활하다 __________
live

2. Complete the conversations using the given words with '오다/어 오다/해 오다' + '았어요'.

챙기다	뛰다	싸다	벌다	돌다

1) A: 칫솔은 __________ ?   B: 아니요. 깜빡했어요.

2) A: 왜 그렇게 땀을 많이 흘렸어요?   B: 늦을까 봐 __________

3) A: 이게 다 뭐예요?   B: 제가 도시락을 __________

4) A: 오늘 돈을 많이 벌었어요?   B: 오늘은 조금밖에 못 __________

5) A: 지금이 몇 시예요?   B: 죄송해요. 차가 너무 막혀서 __________

3. Complete the conversations using '오다/어 오다/해 오다' with the given words and grammar.

훈련하다	연구하다	노력하다	생활하다	참가하다

1) 이 회사에 취직하기 위해 오랫동안 __________ 이제 포기해야 할 것 같아요.   [았다 + 는데]

2) 저는 평생동안 어떻게 하면 외국어를 빨리 습득하고 말할 수 있는 지를 __________   [았다 + 습니다]

3) 어릴 때부터 이런 곳에서 __________ 익숙해요.   [았다 + 기 때문에]

4) 벌써 이 대회에만 __________ 10년째입니다.   [ㄴ 지]

5) 화재 시 대처요령을 __________ 탈출할 수 있었습니다.   [았다 + 기 때문에]

4. Write sentences using '오다/어 오다/해 오다'.

1) __________

2) __________

3) __________

4) __________

5) __________

ㄹ 테다/을 테다
(will so, will but)

No받침 **ㄹ 테다 + 니까**

| 책임지다 | → | 책임질 테니까 | 제가 책임질 테니까 한 번 해 보세요. |
| take responsibility | | I will take the responsibility, so | I will take the responsibility, so try it once. |

| 처리하다 | → | 처리할 테니까 | 제가 처리할 테니까 걱정하지 마세요. |
| handle | | I will handle it, so | I will handle it, so please don't worry. |

받침 **을 테다 + 니까**

| 찾다 | → | 찾을 테니까 | 제가 책임지고 찾을 테니까 믿어 주세요. |
| find | | I will find it, so | I will take the responsibility and find it, so please trust me. |

| 갖다 | → | 갖을 테니까 | 저는 이걸 갖을 테니까 삼촌은 저걸 갖으세요. |
| have | | I will have this, so | I will have this, so you have that. |

No받침 **ㄹ 테다 + ㄴ데**

| 걸리다 | → | 걸릴 텐데 | 시간이 조금 걸릴 텐데 괜찮으세요? |
| take (time) | | it will take, but | It will take a little time, but is it okay? |

| 위험하다 | → | 위험할 텐데 | 위험할 텐데... |
| dangerous | | it will be dangerous | It will be dangerous...(talk to yourself) |

받침 **을 테다 + ㄴ데**

| 작다 | → | 작을 텐데 | 저한테 스몰 사이즈는 작을 텐데... |
| small | | it will be small, but | Small size will be small for me... |

| 많다 | → | 많을 텐데 | 사람이 많을 텐데요? |
| a lot | | there will be a lot | There will be a lot of people? |

Connection

잡다	→	[잡다 + 고 있다 + 을 테다 + 니까]
		제가 잡고 있을 테니까 무서워하지 마세요.
catch, grab, hold		Don't be afraid because I will hold on to it.

도착하다	→	[도착하다 + 했다 + 을 테다 + ㄴ데]
		지금쯤이면 도착했을 텐데 아직 연락이 없네요.
arrive		They should have arrived by now, but I haven't heard from them yet.

Exercises Unit 59

1. Complete the blanks using '이 테다/을 테다' + '니까'.

1) 챙기다	2) 도와주다	3) 들다	4) 마무리하다
look after, pack	help	lift	wrap up

5) 책임지다	6) 맡다	7) 갖고 오다	8) 확인하다
take responsibility	take care of (responsiblity)	bring	check

2. Complete the sentences using '이 테다/을 테다' + '니까', and the given words.

(1)책임지다	(2)갖고 오다	(3)마무리하다	(4)들다	(5)확인하다

1) 제가   걱정하지 마세요.

2) 제가 텐트를   형님은 침낭을 갖고 와 주시겠어요?

3) 제가   과장님은 먼저 들어 가세요.

4) 저는 세탁기를   아저씨는 냉장고를 들어 주세요.

5) 저는 이것을   대리님는 이것을 확인해 주세요.

3. Complete the sentences using '이 테다/을 테다' + '니까'.

1)

2)

3)

4. Complete the blanks using '이 테다/을 테다' + 'ㄴ데'.

1) 알아서 하다	2) 바뀌다	3) 돈이 들다	4) 처리하다
do on one's own	be changed	cost money	handle

5) 불안하다	6) 답답하다	7) 더러워지다	8) 방해되다
anxiety	be frustrated	get dirty	get in the way

5. Complete the sentences using '이 테다/을 테다' + 'ㄴ데', and the words given.

답답하다	더러워지다	들다	알아서 하다	되다

1) 오빠가   무슨 걱정을 그렇게 하세요?

2) 이제 일주일만 지나면 20살이   기분이 어때요?

3) 돈이 많이   뭐 이런 걸 다 사 왔어요?

4) 매일 좁은 곳에서 공부만 하면   선생님은 스트레스를 어떻게 푸세요?

5) 어차피   뭐 하러 청소를 해요.

6. Complete the sentences using '이 테다/을 테다' + 'ㄴ데'.

1)

2)

3)

겠다
(Must be, Will)

No받침 ---------------------------------- 겠다 ----------------------------------

| 비싸다 | → | 비싸**겠다** | A: 명품백을 샀어요. | B: 엄청 비싸겠네요. |
| expensive | | must be expensive | I bought a designer bag. | Oh, it must be really expensive. |

| 짜다 | → | 짜**겠다** | A: 소금을 넣을게요. | B: 짜겠어요. |
| salty | | must be salty | I will put some salt in. | It must be salty. |

받침 ---------------------------------- 겠다 ----------------------------------

| 좋다 | → | 좋**겠다** | A: 여자친구가 생겼어요. | B: 좋겠네요. 축하해요. |
| good | | must be good | I got a girlfriend. | Oh, it must be good. Congratulations. |

| 어렵다 | → | 어렵**겠다** | A: 삼각함수를 풀고 있어요. | B: 어렵겠어요. |
| difficult | | must be difficult | I'm solving a trigonometrical function. | It must be difficult. |

No받침 ---------------------------------- 겠다 ----------------------------------

| 내다 | → | 내**겠다** | A: 이력서를 냈어요? | B: 내일까지 내겠습니다. |
| submit, pay | | will submit | Did you submit the résumé? | I will submit it by tomorrow. |

| 확인하다 | → | 확인하**겠다** | A: 누가 체크할 거예요? | A: 제가 확인하겠습니다. |
| check | | will check | Who is going to check it? | I will check it. |

받침 ---------------------------------- 겠다 ----------------------------------

| 들다 | → | 들**겠다** | A: 저는 20kg을 들 수 있어요. | B: 제 여자친구도 20kg은 들겠네요. |
| lift | | will lift | I can lift 20kg. | Oh, even my girlfriend will lift 20kg. |

| 돈이 들다 | → | 돈이 들**겠다** | A: 세탁기가 고장났어요. | B: 또 돈이 들겠네요. |
| cost money | | will cost money | The laundry machine is broken. | Oh, it will cost money again. |

Connection ----------------------------------

[하다 + ㄹ 수 있다 + 겠다 + 어요]

| 최선을 다하다 | A: 어려워 보이는데, 할 수 있겠어요? | B: 네. 최선을 다하겠습니다. |
| do one's best | It looks difficult, but will you be able to do it? | Yes. I will do my best. |

Exercises Unit 60

1. Complete the blanks using '겠다 + 어요'.

1) 맛있다 taste good	2) 힘들다 hard	3) 좋다 good	4) 아프다 hurt, sick
5) 미치다 crazy	6) 죽다 die	7) 어렵다 difficult	8) 피곤하다 tired

2. Complete the conversations using '겠다 + 어요' with the appropriate words.

어렵다	피곤하다	좋다	미치다	아프다

1) A: 저는 어제 시험공부를 하느라 밤을 샜어요.　　　B:

2) A: 어제 엄마한테 용돈을 받았어요.　　　B:

3) A: 책상에 이마를 부딪쳐서 멍이 들었어요.　　　B:

3. Complete the blanks using '겠다 + 네요'.

1) 바쁘다 busy	2) 기쁘다 glad	3) 재미있다 fun	4) 시원하다 cool
5) 한가하다 free (not busy)	6) 짜증나다 annoyed	7) 따뜻하다 warm	8) 쌀쌀하다 chilly

4. Complete the conversations using '겠다 + 네요' with the appropriate words.

쌀쌀하다	바쁘다	따뜻하다	기쁘다	한가하다

1) A: 저는 내일 일도 해야 되고 운동도 해야 되고 숙제도 해야 돼요.　B:

2) A: 제 아내가 임신했대요.　　　B:

3) A: 내일은 비가 온대요.　　　B:

5. Complete the blanks using '겠다 + 습니다'.

1) 종료하다 exit	2) 드리다 give	3) 공개하다 make public	4) 사과하다 apologize
5) 해결하다 solve	6) 처리하다 handle	7) 교육하다 educate	8) 제출하다 submit

6. Complete the conversations using '겠다 + 습니다' with the appropriate words.

드리다	해결하다	따뜻하다	제출하다	한가하다

1) A: 이력서를 제출했나요?　　　　　　　B: 아니요. 1시까지

2) A: 저는 새 핸드폰이 필요해요.　　　　　B: 15만원에

3) A: 누가 처리할 거예요?　　　　　　　B: 제가

UNIT 61 | 면 할수록
(the more the...)

          ~면 ~ㄹ수록

크다 → 크면 클수록   크면 클수록 좋아요.
big   the bigger it is   The bigger the better.

비싸다 → 비싸면 비쌀수록   물건이 비싸면 비쌀수록 더 잘 팔려요.
expensive   the more expensive it is   The more expensive the item is, the better it sells.

          으면 을수록

키가 작다 → 키가 작으면 작을수록   키가 작으면 작을수록 유리해요.
short   the shorter it is   The shorter the more advantageous.

많다 → 많으면 많을수록   아는 사람이 많으면 많을수록 도움이 될 거예요.
many   more and more   The more people you know, it will help.

          ~면 ~ㄹ수록

보다 → 보면 볼수록   보면 볼수록 매력이 있어요.
look   the more one looks   The more I look at it, the more attractive it is.

하다 → 하면 할수록   하면 할수록 어려워요
do   the more one does it   The more I do it, the more diffucult it is.

          으면 을수록

나이를 먹다 → 나이를 먹으면 먹을수록   나이를 먹으면 먹을수록 외로워져요.
grow old   as you get older   As I get older, I feel lonely.

읽다 → 읽으면 읽을수록   그 책은 읽으면 읽을수록 감동적이에요.
read   the more I read   The more I read the book, the more touching it is.

연습하다 → 연습을 많이 하면 할수록 실력이 빨리 늘 거예요.
practice   The more you practice, the faster you are going to improve your ability.

Exercises Unit 61

1. Complete the blanks using '면 ㄹ수록/으면 을수록'.

1) 빠르다 ___________   2) 많다 ___________   3) 게으르다 ___________   4) 밝다 ___________
fast   many   lazy   bright

5) 크다 ___________   6) 작다 ___________   7) 높다 ___________   8) 낮다 ___________
big   small   high   low

2. Complete the conversations using '면 ㄹ수록 좋아요/으면 을수록 좋아요' with the words given.

밝다	높다	많다	빠르다	크다

1) A: 여권이 언제 필요해요?   B: ___________

2) A: 얼마나 필요해요?   B: ___________

3) A: 얼마나 밝게 해 드릴까요?   B: ___________

3. Complete the blanks using '면 ㄹ수록/으면 을수록'.

1) 지나다 ___________   2) 생각하다 ___________   3) 실패하다 ___________   4) 나누다 ___________
pass (time)   think   fail   share

5) 보다 ___________   6) 도전하다 ___________   7) 파다 ___________   8) 숨을 쉬다 ___________
look, see, watch   challenge   dig   breathe

4. Complete the sentences using '면 ㄹ수록/으면 을수록' with the words given.

생각하다	하다	보다	나누다	지나다

1) 시간이 ___________ 상하니까 되도록이면 빨리 드세요.

2) ___________ 기분이 나빠요.

3) 게임은 ___________ 더 하고 싶어지는 것 같아요.

4) ___________ 행복해져요.

5) ___________ 정이 드네요.

5. Write sentences using '면 ㄹ수록/으면 을수록'.

1) ___________

2) ___________

3) ___________

4) ___________

5) ___________

Final Test 1

1. 혹시 정수기도 인터넷에서 (   )?   **Unit 1**
   A 팔나요   B 팔으나요   C 파나요   D 판가요

2. 혹시 지금 여기로 올 수 (   )?   **Unit 1**
   A 있나요   B 있으나요   C 이나요   D 인나요

3. 그 사람은 동양 사람(   ), 아니면 서양 사람(   )?   **Unit 2**
   A 이나요   B 이가요   C 인가요   D 인나요

4. 여기에서 공항까지 (   ), (   )? .   **Unit 2**
   A 먼가요, 가까운가요   B 멀가요, 가깝은가요   C 먼가요, 가깝은가요   D 멀가요, 가까운가요

5. 사람의 머리카락은 몇 개(   )?   **Unit 3**
   A 을까요   B 일까요   C 까요   D ㄹ까요

6. 선풍기가 고장났는데 새로 사는 것이 (   ), 아니면 고치는 것이 (   )?   **Unit 3**
   A 좋을까요   B 좋까요   C 좋아할까요   D 좋할까요

7. 친구한테 빌려준 돈을 못 (   ) 걱정이에요 .   **Unit 4**
   A 발까 봐   B 발을까 봐   C 받을까 봐   D 받까 봐

8. 어려 (   ) 화장을 했어요.   **Unit 4**
   A 까 봐   B 볼까 봐   C 보을까 봐   D 보일까 봐

9. 한국어를 다 알아 듣는데 (   )했어요.   **Unit 5**
   A 몰르는 척   B 모르는 척   C 모르은 척   D 모를 척

10. 힘들어도 (   )하지 마세요.   **Unit 5**
   A 힘들 척   B 힘든 척   C 힘드 척   D 힘드는 척

11. 길에서 전 남자친구를 봤는데 (   )했어요.   **Unit 5**
   A 못 봔 척   B 못 볼 척   C 못 보는 척   D 못 본 척

12. 하마터면 큰일 (   )했어요.　　　　　　　　　　**Unit 6**

    A 나다　　　B 났다　　　C 날 뻔　　　D 나를 뻔

13. 앞 사람이랑 부딪(   )했는데 다행히 안 부딪쳤어요.　　**Unit 6**

    A 치일 뻔　　　B 칠 뻔　　　C 치를 뻔　　　D 치는 척

14. 오늘부터 다이어트를 (   ) 마음먹었어요.　　**Unit 7**

    A 하기로　　　B 기로　　　C 하기　　　D 기

15. 100만 원을 모으(   ) 결심했어요.　　　　**Unit 7**

    A 하기로　　　B 기로　　　C 기　　　D 하기

16. 9월부터 친구하고 운동 (   ) 했어요.　　　**Unit 7**

    A 하고　　　B 기로　　　C 하기로　　　D 하기

17. 요즘 살이 찐 것 같아서 살을 (   ) 결정했어요.　　**Unit 7**

    A 더하기로　　　B 빼기로　　　C 나누기로　　　D 곱하기로

18. 더 이상 친구를 놀리(   ) 약속했어요.　　　**Unit 7**

    A 기로　　　B 지 않기로　　　C 안 기로　　　D 하기로

19. 이 친구는 제가 어릴 때 짝사랑(   ) 친구예요.　　**Unit 8**

    A 던　　　B 할　　　C 할 것이던　　　D 하던

20. (   )것을 마저 하고 갈게요.　　　　**Unit 8**

    A 하던　　　B 먹던　　　C 가던　　　D 살던

21. 제가 (   ) 것이에요(거예요).　　　**Unit 8**

    A 쓰든　　　B 쓰고 있다　　　C 쓰고 있던　　　D 써던

22. 대학생 때 (   ) 내용이에요.　　　　**Unit 8**

    A 배웠던　　　B 배우고 있는　　　C 배웠던 것　　　D 배웊던

23. 저는 5년 전에 영업사원(   ).   **Unit 9**
   A 이에요   B 였어요   C 이었었어요   D 이요

24. 옛날에 할머니가 그런 말씀을 자주 (   ).   **Unit 9**
   A 하셨었어요   B 하시었었어요   C 하세요   D 하셔었었어요

25. 오늘은 1일이 아니라 31일(   )?   **Unit 10**
   A 던데요   B 이던데요   C 더라고요   D 던데

26. 문제가 생각보다 복잡(   )?   **Unit 10**
   A 하던데요   B 던데요   C 이던데요   D 던걸요

27. A: 혹시 진호 씨를 봤어요? B: 네. 1층에서 봤어요. 커피를 마시고 (   )?   **Unit 10**
   A 이던데요   B 던데요   C 있든데요   D 있던데요

28. 오늘이 휴일인 줄 알았는데 내일(   ).   **Unit 11**
   A 더라고요   B 더래요   C 이더라고요   D 이라면서요

29. 필리핀, 보라카이에 가 봤는데 엄청 평화롭(   ).   **Unit 11**
   A 하더라고요   B 더라고요   C 이더라고요   D 워더라고요

30. 그 사람은 환경을 중요하게 생각해서 심지어 일회용 종이컵(   ) 안 쓰더라고요.   **Unit 12**
   A 아도   B 어도   C 도   D 해도

31. 아무리 노력(   ) 잘 안 돼요.   **Unit 12**
   A 도   B 어도   C 아도   D 해도

32. 슬(   ) 울지 말아요.   **Unit 12**
   A 퍼도   B 프도   C 프해도   D 파도

33. 이제 보고 (　　　　) 못 봐요.　　　　　　　　　　　　　　　Unit 12
　　A 싶도　　　　B 싶어도　　　　C 싶아도　　　　D 싶지도

34. 일이 지겹(　　　　)으세요?　　　　　　　　　　　　　　　Unit 13
　　A 지도　　　　B 도　　　　C 지도 않　　　　D 지도 못

35. 면접을 볼 때 너무 긴장해서 말(　　　　)했어요.　　　　　Unit 13
　　A 도 못　　　　B 지도 않　　　　C 해지도 못　　　　D 도 않

36. 아무리 전문가(　　　　) 해결할 수 없는 문제가 있어요.　Unit 14
　　A 드라도　　　　B 더라고　　　　C 더라도　　　　D 이드라도

37. 힘들고 어렵(　　　　) 절대 포기하지 마세요.　　　　　　Unit 14
　　A 더라도　　　　B 이더라도　　　　C 워더라도　　　　D 워드라도

38. 갑자기 날씨가 흐려지(　　　　) 비가 내리기 시작했어요.　Unit 15
　　A 드니　　　　B 던데　　　　C 더니　　　　D 으더니

39. 어떤 사람이 갑자기 옷을 벗(　　　　) 소리를 질렀어요.　Unit 15
　　A 으드니　　　　B 드니　　　　C 으더니　　　　D 더니

40. 요즘 들어 부쩍 덩치가 (　　　　) 것 같아요.　　　　　　Unit 16
　　A 크진　　　　B 커진　　　　C 카진　　　　D 쿠진

41. 요즘 연애하세요? 얼굴이 (　　　　).　　　　　　　　　　Unit 16
　　A 좋아지다　　　　B 좋어지다　　　　C 좋아졌어요　　　　D 좋어졌어요

42. 수업이 몇 시에 끝나(　　　　) 아세요?　　　　　　　　　Unit 17
　　A 인지　　　　B 을지　　　　C 던지　　　　D 는지

43. 무슨 소리(   ) 이해돼요?   **Unit 17**

   A 인지   B 는지   C 을지   D 지

44. 그 신발을 어디에서 (   ) 말해 주시면 안 돼요?   **Unit 17**

   A 구할 수 있는지   B 구하고 싶은지   C 구해 주고   D 구할 때

45. 어떻게 (   ) 보여 주세요.   **Unit 17**

   A 만들을지   B 만든지   C 만들어   D 만들는지

46. 보통 제가 유학생(   ), 직장인(   ) 잘 모르더라고요.   **Unit 18**

   A 인지   B 은지   C 는지   D 아닌지

47. 인터넷이 (   ), (   ) 확인해 봤어요?   **Unit 18**

   A 빠르는지, 느리는지   B 빠르는지, 느린지   C 빠른지, 느리는지   D 빠른지, 느린지

48. 오늘 몇 시에 어디에서 만날 (   ) 결정해서 알려 주세요.   **Unit 18**

   A 거인지   B 것는지   C 것인지   D 거는지

49. 임신(   ) 얼마나 됐어요?   **Unit 19**

   A 지   B ㄴ 지   C 한 지   D 하는 지

50. 저는 영어를 (   ) 10년쯤 됐는데 아직도 못해요.   **Unit 19**

   A 배운지   B 배원지   C 배우지   D 배우는지

51. 한국에서 (   ) 벌써 3년이나 됐어요.   **Unit 19**

   A 생활하는지   B 생활했는지   C 생활핸 지   D 생활한 지

52. 그냥 가지고 가지 마세요. 유료(   ) 몰라요.   **Unit 20**

   A 인줄도   B 일지도   C 을지도   D 할지도

53. 내년에 호주로 (　　　　) 지도 몰라서 영어를 공부해야 돼요.　　　　**Unit 20**
　　A 이사 갈　　　B 이사 간　　　C 이사 가는　　　D 이사 가일

54. 일이 너무 단순해서 (　　　　) 지도 모르지만 최선을 다해 주세요.　　　　**Unit 20**
　　A 지겹을　　　B 지겨울　　　C 지겹우는　　　D 지겨운

55. 너무 어려 보여서 학생(　　　　) 줄 알았어요.　　　　**Unit 21**
　　A 은　　　B 이는　　　C 인　　　D 는

56. 날씨가 (　　　　) 줄 알고 반팔 티셔츠를 입고 왔는데 너무 추워요.　　　　**Unit 21**
　　A 더운　　　B 덥운　　　C 추운　　　D 춥운

57. A: 오늘 지선 씨는 아파서 못 온대요. B: 또요? (　　　　) 줄 알았어요.　　　　**Unit 21**
　　A 그런　　　B 그러는　　　C 그럼　　　D 그럴

58. 오늘부터 방학(　　　　) 모르고 학교에 나왔어요.　　　　**Unit 22**
　　A 이는 줄　　　B 인 줄　　　C 일 줄　　　D 은 줄

59. 상황이 그렇게 (　　　　) 줄 몰랐어요.　　　　**Unit 22**
　　A 심각하는 줄　　　B 심각한 줄　　　C 심각했 줄　　　D 심각하은 줄

60. 문자가 (　　　　) 모르고 있었어요.　　　　**Unit 22**
　　A 온 줄　　　B 완 줄　　　C 오는 줄　　　D 와는 줄

61. A: 제가 왜 참아야 돼요? B: 어른(　　　　).　　　　**Unit 23**
　　A 잖아요　　　B 은 잖아요　　　C 는 잖아요　　　D 이잖아요

62. A: 청소를 안 할 거예요? B: 안 보여요? 지금 하고 있(　　　　).　　　　**Unit 23**
　　A 잖아요　　　B 으 잖아요　　　C 이 잖아요　　　D 는 잖아요

63. 왜 안 했어요? 제가 어제 하라고 말했(　　　　　).　　　　　　　**Unit 23**
　　A 은 잖아요　　　B 어 잖아요　　　C 잖아요　　　D 이 잖아요

64. A: 이게 다 뭐예요?　B: 선물이에요. 오늘은 좀 특별한 날(　　　　　).　**Unit 24**
　　A 거든요　　　B 이거든요　　　C 어 거든요　　　D 은 거든요

65. A: 둘이 왜 말을 안 해요? 분위기가 안 좋네요. B: 둘이 (　　　　　).　**Unit 24**
　　A 싸우거든요　　　B 싸웠거든요　　　C 싸웠거든요　　　D 싸운 거든요

66. A: 벌써 표가 매진됐어요. B: 요즘 인기가 아주 (　　　　　).　　**Unit 24**
　　A 많이거든요　　　B 많은거든요　　　C 많거든요　　　D 많다거든요

67. A: 오늘이 성훈 씨의 생일이에요. B: 내일(　　　　　)?　　　　　**Unit 25**
　　A 인데요　　　B 은데요　　　C 는데요　　　D 데요

68. A: 정답은 0이에요. B: (　　　　　)?　　　　　　　　　　　　**Unit 25**
　　A 아니다　　　B 아닌데요　　　C 아니는데요　　　D 아니은데요

69. A: 햄버거를 안 좋아하시죠? B: (　　　　　)?　　　　　　　　**Unit 25**
　　A 좋아하시는데요　　　B 좋아하는데요　　　C 좋아한데요　　　D 좋아해는데요

70. (　　　　　)는 쉽지만 (　　　　　)는 쉽지 않죠.　　　　　　　**Unit 26**
　　A 말하기, 실천하기　　B 말하다, 실천하다　　C 말하는 것, 실천하는 것　　D 말, 실천

71. 한 달 전부터 영어로 일기를 쓰(　　　　　).　　　　　　　　　**Unit 26**
　　A 었어요　　　B 기 시작해요　　　C 기 시작할 거예요　　　D 기 시작했어요

72. 요새 먹고 살(　　　　　).　　　　　　　　　　　　　　　　**Unit 26**
　　A 는 것이 힘들어요　　　B 기 힘들어요　　　C 힘들어요　　　D 는 것은 힘들어요

73. 습관을 고치( )은 어려운 것이에요.　　　　　　　　　　**Unit 26**
　　A 기　　　B 는 것　　　C 은 것　　　D 는 방법

74. 흔( )이에요.　　　　　　　　　　　　　　　　　　**Unit 27**
　　A 은 일　　　B 한 일　　　C 운 것　　　D 는 것

75. 취미로 하( ) 것이에요.　　　　　　　　　　　　　　**Unit 27**
　　A 은　　　B 는　　　C 이　　　D 가

76. 제가 갖고 싶( )은 인형인데 엄마가 로보트를 사 오셨어요.　**Unit 27**
　　A 는 것　　　B 은 것　　　C 운 것　　　D 어 것

77. 이게 보기( ) 꽤 어려워요.　　　　　　　　　　　　　**Unit 28**
　　A 가다　　　B 먹다　　　C 보다　　　D 사다

78. 전철로 갈아타( ) 버스로 갈아타는 것이 더 나아요.　　　**Unit 28**
　　A 는 것보다　　　B 은 것보다　　　C 것보다　　　D 보다

79. ( ) 기술을 어디에서 배웠어요?　　　　　　　　　　　**Unit 29**
　　A 그렇다　　　B 그렇게　　　C 그런　　　D 그럼

80. ( ) 그림이 제일 마음에 들어요?　　　　　　　　　　　**Unit 29**
　　A 어떻다　　　B 어떻게　　　C 어떤　　　D 어때

81. ( ) 옷을 구하고 싶은데 어디에서 살 수 있는지 모르겠어요.　**Unit 29**
　　A 이렇게　　　B 이런　　　C 이렇지만　　　D 이렇듯이

82. 벌에 ( ).　　　　　　　　　　　　　　　　　　　　**Unit 30**
　　A 쏘다　　　B 쏘여다　　　C 쏘였어요　　　D 쐈어요

83. 경찰한테 (　　　　).   **Unit 30**
　　A 잡았어요　　　B 잡혔어요　　　C 잡아요　　　D 자워요

84. 벌레한테 (　　　　).   **Unit 30**
　　A 물렸어요　　　B 물었어요　　　C 물어요　　　D 무렸어요

85. 와이파이가 (　　　　).   **Unit 30**
　　A 끊겨요　　　B 끊켜요　　　C 끊어요　　　D 끊었어요

86. 경기가 (　　　　).   **Unit 31**
　　A 시작돼었어요　　　B 시작됐어요　　　C 시작이에요　　　D 시작뒜어요

87. 1,000원을 결제했는데 카드를 확인해 보니까 10,000원이(　　　　).   **Unit 31**
　　A 결제요　　　B 결제했어요　　　C 결재돼요　　　D 결제됐어요

88. 아이디를 해킹(　　　　).   **Unit 31**
　　A 됐어요　　　B 돼요　　　C 당했어요　　　D 되다

89. 일본어 학원에 (　　　　).   **Unit 32**
　　A 다녀게 됬어요　　　B 다녀게 됐어요　　　C 다니게 됬어요　　　D 다니게 됐어요

90. 해외여행을 하면서 많은 것들을 (　　　　).   **Unit 32**
　　A 경험하게 됬어요　　B 경험하게 되었어요　　C 경험해게 됬어요　　D 경험해게 되었어요

91. 요즘 세상은 인터넷으로 (　　　　).   **Unit 33**
　　A 연결해 있어요　　　B 연결하 있어요　　　C 연결돼 있어요　　　D 연결되 있어요

92. 지금 빌딩 앞에 (　　　　).   **Unit 33**
　　A 서 있어요　　　B 서어 있어요　　　C 서아 있어요　　　D 서해 있어요

93. 부탁이니까 (　　　　)지 마세요.	**Unit 34**
　A 짜증나게　　　B 짜증나게 하다　　　C 짜증나게 하　　　D 짜증나게 해

94. 동생한테 심부름을 (　　　　).	**Unit 34**
　A 해게 했어요　　　B 시켜 만들었어요　　　C 시킸어요　　　D 시켰어요

95. 조금만 (　　　　) 말씀해 주시겠어요?	**Unit 35**
　A 천천이　　　B 천천히　　　C 천천게　　　D 천천하히

96. 너무 어렵네요. 좀 더 (　　　　) 설명해 주실래요?	**Unit 35**
　A 간단한　　　B 간단히　　　C 간단하게　　　D 간단하

97. A: 날씨가 좋네요. B: 날씨가 (　　　　)?	**Unit 36**
　A 춥다고요　　　B 추워다고요　　　C 추운다고요　　　D 춥다고 해요

98. A: 안 갈 거예요. B: 안 (　　　　)?	**Unit 36**
　A 가시다고요　　　B 가시는다고 해요　　　C 가신다고요　　　D 가신다고 해요

99. A: 선생님은 안 (　　　　)?	**Unit 36**
　A 온대요　　　B 오신대요　　　C 완대요　　　D 와신대요

100. A: 그 사람은 어제 떠났어요. B: 어제요? 벌써 (　　　　)?	**Unit 37**
　A 떠난다고요　　　B 떠난다고 해요　　　C 떠났다고요　　　D 떠났다고 해요

101. 한 시간전에 출발(　　　　　　　) 아직 도착 안 했나요?	**Unit 37**
　A 했다고 해서　　　B 했다고 했는데　　　C 한다고 해서　　　D 한다고 하는데

102. A: 차를 바꿀 거예요. B: 차를 (　　　　　　　)?	**Unit 38**
　A 바꿀 거라고요　　　B 바꿔라고요　　　C 바꾼 거라고요　　　D 바뀔 거라고요

103. 제가 친구한테 내일부터 다이어트를 (　　　　). **Unit 38**
A 하는 거라고 했어요　　　B 할 거라고 했어요　　　C 할 거라고 할 거예요　　　D 한 거라고 했어요

104. A: 몇 살이세요? B: 몇 살(　　　　)? **Unit 39**
A 냐고요　　　B 이냐고요　　　C 이시냐고요　　　D 시냐고요

105. A: 염색하셨어요? B: 염색(　　　　)? **Unit 39**
A 하냐고요　　　B 하셨냐고요　　　C 했냐고요　　　D 이냐고요

106. A: 사실 저는 남자친구가 있어요. B: 뭐(　　　　)? **Unit 40**
A 냐고요　　　B 다고요　　　C 거라고요　　　D 라고요

107. A: 가세요. B: 네? A: 가(　　　　)! **Unit 40**
A 라고요　　　B 으라고요　　　C 라고 해요　　　D 으라고 해요

108. 안녕하세요. 저는 송원(　　　　) 합니다. **Unit 40**
A 라고　　　B 이라고　　　C 라고요　　　D 이라고요

109. A: 우리 말을 놓을까요? B: 말을 (　　　　)? **Unit 41**
A 놓는다고요　　　B 놓을 거라고요　　　C 놓자고요　　　D 놓냐고요

110. 여자친구한테 결혼하(　　　　) 했어요. **Unit 41**
A 자고　　　B 시자고　　　C 기로　　　D 기를

111. 사장님께 기회(　　　　) 말했어요. **Unit 42**
A 을 달라고　　　B 를 달라고　　　C 달라고　　　D 달라고 해서

112. 친구가 (　　　　)해서 도와줬어요. **Unit 42**
A 돕어 달라고　　　B 도워 달라고　　　C 도와 달라고　　　D 돕아 달라고

113. 오늘 왜 회사에 가요? 쉬는 날(　　　　　).   **Unit 43**

A 다면서요　　　　B 한다면서요　　　　C 라면서요　　　　D 이라면서요

114. 헬스장에 안 가세요? 오늘부터 운동(　　　　　).   **Unit 43**

A 면서요　　　　B 한다면서요　　　　C 하는다면서요　　　　D 했다면서요

115. 음악을 (　　　　　) 운전하고 있었어요.   **Unit 44**

A 듣면서　　　　B 듣으면서　　　　C 들면서　　　　D 들으면서

116. 다 먹지도 못(　　　　　) 왜 이렇게 많이 시켰어요?   **Unit 44**

A 하면서　　　　B 하으면서　　　　C 해면서　　　　D 해으면서

117. A: 무슨 상처예요? B: 어릴 때 계단을 내려가(　　　　　) 계단에서 굴렀어요.   **Unit 45**

A 다가　　　　B 어다가　　　　C 아다가　　　　D 해다가

118. A: 이게 다 뭐예요? B: 꽃 가게를 지나가(　　　　　) 여자친구한테 주려고 샀어요.   **Unit 45**

A 갔다가　　　　B 시다가　　　　C 갈 때　　　　D 다가

119. A: 왜 그렇게 땀을 흘려요? B: 지각할까 봐 뛰어(　　　　　) 땀이 많이 났어요.   **Unit 46**

A 가느라고　　　　B 오느라고　　　　C 왔느라고　　　　D 갔느라고

120. A: 왜 제 문자를 무시해요? B: 죄송해요. 아빠랑 전화를 (　　　　　) 문자를 못 봤어요.   **Unit 46**

A 받느라고　　　　B 하느라고　　　　C 통화하느라고　　　　D 끊느라고

121. A: 처음으로 요리를 해 봤는데 어때요? B: 먹(　　　　　).   **Unit 47**

A 만하다　　　　B 을 만하다　　　　C 만해요　　　　D 을 만해요

122. A: 스페인에 가 봤다면서요? 어땠어요? B: (　　　　　).   **Unit 47**

A 가을 만해요　　　　B 가 볼 만해요　　　　C 가 보고 싶어요　　　　D 가 볼 만해요

123. 옛날 거라서 느리(   ) 아직 쓸 만해요.   **Unit 48**
    A 긴 하고   B 긴 한데   C 긴 하는데   D 긴 하다

124. A: 시험 결과가 궁금하지 않으세요? B: 궁금(   ).   **Unit 48**
    A 하긴 해요   B 해긴 해요   C 긴 해요   D 긴 궁금해요

125. 클럽에 들어갔는데 아무도 없(   ) 바로 나왔어요.   **Unit 49**
    A 길래   B 으길래   C 어길래   D 하길래

126. 친구가 (   )길래 제가 아는 사람을 소개해 줬어요.   **Unit 50**
    A 외롭   B 외로워하   C 외로와하   D 외로운

127. 그런 말을 (   ) 얼마나 힘이 빠지는지 아세요?   **Unit 51**
    A 듣 때마다   B 들 때마다   C 듣을 때마다   D 들을 때마다

128. 해가 (   ) 운동장에서 축구를 했어요.   **Unit 52**
    A 질 때까지   B 지을 때까지   C 이길 때까지   D 지울 때까지

129. 그 사람이 그런 소리를 (   ) 없어요.   **Unit 53**
    A 었을 리가   B 았을 리가   C 했을 리가   D 리가

130. 거짓말(   ) 없어요.   **Unit 53**
    A 리가   B 일 리가   C 을 리가   D 울 리가

131. 수업시간에 계속 핸드폰을 사용하면 압수(   ) 없어요.   **Unit 54**
    A 밖에   B 을 수 밖에   C 할 수밖에   D 수 밖에

132. 컴퓨터가 느려져서 파일을 (   ) 버렸어요.   **Unit 55**
    A 삭제   B 삭제해   C 삭제하   D 삭제어

133. 짐이 많아서 사물함에 (　　　　　).　　　　　　　　　　　**Unit 56**
　　A 놓었어요　　　B 놓왔어요　　　C 넣어 놓었어요　　　D 넣어 놓았어요

134. 분실물 센터에 보관(　　　　　　) 찾아가세요.　　　　　　**Unit 56**
　　A 해 놓았으니까　　　B 놓았으니까　　　C 해 놓었으니까　　　D 놓었으니까

135. 시간이 다 (　　　　　　) 서두르세요.　　　　　　　　　　**Unit 57**
　　A 되가니까　　　B 되어 가니까　　　C 되해 가니까　　　D 돼어 가니까

136. 이 분야에서 20년 동안 일(　　　　　　) 다양한 사람들을 만나 봤어요.　　　**Unit 58**
　　A 오면서　　　B 어 오면서　　　C 아 오면서　　　D 해 오면서

137. 텐트는 제가 가져(　　　　　　) 안 가져오셔도 돼요.　　　**Unit 59**
　　A 갈 테니까　　　B 갈 텐데　　　C 갈 테다　　　D 갈게요

138. 이제 곧 여름이 (　　　　　　) 에어컨 청소는 해 놓았어요?　　　**Unit 59**
　　A 될 테니까　　　B 될 텐데　　　C 됄 테니까　　　D 됄 텐데

139. A: 할 수 있는 사람이 있나요? B: 제가 한 번 해 (　　　　　　).　　　**Unit 60**
　　A 보겠습니다　　　B 봐겠습니다　　　C 보겠다　　　D 봐겠다

140. 생각(　　　　　　) 화가 나요.　　　　　　　　　　**Unit 61**
　　A 나면 날수록　　　B 하면 할수록　　　C 해면 핼수록　　　D 으면 을수록

141. 웃(　　　　　　) 젊어진대요.　　　　　　　　　　**Unit 61**
　　A 면 웃을수록　　　B 어면 웃을수록　　　C 으면 웃을수록　　　D 우면 웃을수록

142. (　　　　　　) 짜증이 나서 못 참겠어요.　　　　　　**Unit 61**
　　A 듣으면 듣을수록　　　B 들으면 들을수록　　　C 들면 들을수록　　　D 들면 들수록

Final Test 2

1. Write a sentence. Use '나요'.

2. Write a sentence. Use '인가요?'.

3. Write a sentence. Use 'ㄴ가요/은가요?'.

4. Write a sentence. Use 'ㄹ까요/을까요?'.

5. Write a sentence. Use 'ㄹ까 봐/을까 봐'.

6. Write a sentence. Use 'ㄴ 척하다/은 척하다'.

7. Write a sentence. Use 'ㄹ 뻔하다/을 뻔하다'.

8. Write a sentence. Use '기로 하다'.

9. Write a sentence. Use '기로 결정하다'.

10. Write a sentence. Use '기로 결심하다'.

11. Write a sentence. Use '기로 약속하다'.

12. Write a sentence. Use '던'.

13. Write a sentence. Use '였었다/이었었다'.

14. Write a sentence. Use 'ㅆ었다/었었다/했었다'.

15. Write a sentence. Use '던데요'.

16. Write a sentence. Use '더라고요'.

17. Write a sentence. Use '심지어 ~도/어도/해도'.

18. Write a sentence. Use '지도 않다'.

19. Write a sentence. Use '지도 못하다'.

20. Write a sentence. Use '아무리 ~더라도'.

21. Write a sentence. Use '갑자기 ~더니'.

22. Write a sentence. Use '지다/어지다/해지다'.

23. Write a sentence. Use '지다/어지다/해지다'.

24. Write a sentence. Use '는지'.

---

25. Write a sentence. Use '인지/ㄴ지/은지/는지'.

---

26. Write a sentence. Use 'ㄴ 지 얼마나 되다/은 지 얼마나 되다'.

---

27. Write a sentence. Use 'ㄹ지도/을지도'.

---

28. Write a sentence. Use '인 줄 알다/ㄴ 줄 알다/은 줄 알다'.

---

29. Write a sentence. Use '인 줄 모르다/ㄴ 줄 모르다/은 줄 모르다/는 줄 모르다'.

---

30. Write a sentence. Use '잖아요/이잖아요'.

---

31. Write a sentence. Use '왜냐하면 ~거든요/이거든요'.

---

32. Write a sentence. Use '는데요?'.

---

33. Write a sentence. Use '기'.

---

34. Write a sentence. Use '는 것'.

---

35. Write a sentence. Use '것'.

---

36. Write a sentence. Use '보다'.

37. Write a sentence. Use '이렇다, 그렇다, 저렇다, 어떻다'.

38. Write a sentence. Use '이, 히, 리, 기'.

39. Write a sentence. Use '되다.

40. Write a sentence. Use '당하다'.

41. Write a sentence. Use '게 되다'.

42. Write a sentence. Use '있다/어 있다/해 있다'.

43. Write a sentence. Use '게 하다'.

44. Write a sentence. Use '게, 히'.

45. Write a sentence. Use '다고요'.

46. Write a sentence. Use '다고 하다'.

47. Write a sentence. Use '했다고요'.

48. Write a sentence. Use '했다고 하다'.

49. Write a sentence. Use '거라고요'.

50. Write a sentence. Use '거라고 하다'.

51. Write a sentence. Use '냐고요'.

52. Write a sentence. Use '냐고 하다'.

53. Write a sentence. Use '라고요'.

54. Write a sentence. Use '라고 하다'.

55. Write a sentence. Use '자고요'.

56. Write a sentence. Use '자고 하다'.

57. Write a sentence. Use '달라고요'.

58. Write a sentence. Use '달라고 하다'.

59. Write a sentence. Use 'ㄴ다면서/는다면서'.

60. Write a sentence. Use '면서/으면서'.

61. Write a sentence. Use '다가'.

62. Write a sentence. Use '느라고'.

63. Write a sentence. Use 'ㄹ 만하다/을 만하다'.

64. Write a sentence. Use '기는 하다'.

65. Write a sentence. Use '길래'.

66. Write a sentence. Use '하다/어하다/해하다'.

67. Write a sentence. Use 'ㄹ 때마다/을 때마다'.

68. Write a sentence. Use 'ㄹ 때까지/을 때까지'.

69. Write a sentence. Use 'ㄹ 리가 없다/을 리가 없다'.

70. Write a sentence. Use 'ㄹ 수밖에 없다/을 수밖에 없다'.

71. Write a sentence. Use '버리다/어 버리다/해 버리다'.

72. Write a sentence. Use '놓다/어 놓다/해 놓다'.

73. Write a sentence. Use '가다/어 가다/해 가다'.

74. Write a sentence. Use '오다/어 오다/해 오다'.

75. Write a sentence. Use 'ㄹ 테니까/을 테니까'.

76. Write a sentence. Use 'ㄹ 텐데/을 텐데'.

77. Write a sentence. Use '겠다'.

78. Write a sentence. Use '~면 ~ㄹ수록'.

No받침 Verbs

ㄱ

가리다	cover, be picky
갈아타다	transfer to
감기에 걸리다	catch a cold
감추다	hide
갔다 오다	go and come back
개기다	defy
걱정을 끼치다	cause anxiety
건드리다	touch, nudge
건지다	fish something out
걸리다	be caught, be hung, take
걸치다	put on
겨루다	compete
견디다	put up with
결과가 나오다	release results
겹치다	overlap
고르다	choose, select, pick
골프를 치다	play golf
기대다	lean on
기르다	raise
길을 건너다	cross the street
김치를 담그다	make kimchi
까다	peel
꺼내다	take out, bring up
껴안다	hug
꼬시다	hit on
꾸미다	decorate
꿈을 꾸다	have a dream
꿈을 이루다	achieve a dream
꿈을 펼치다	follow a dream
꿈이 이루어지다	a dream comes true
꿰매다	sew
끈을 매다	tie the strings
끝내주다	wonderful, super
기억나다	remember
기울이다	tilt

ㄴ

나누다	divide
나오다	come out
날씨가 풀리다	the weather gets warm
낯을 가리다	shy around strangers
내려가다	go down
내려오다	come down
내리다	get off
넘어가다	cross, pass
넘어오다	come cross
넘어지다	fall down
넘치다	overflow
넥타이를 매다	wear a tie
노래를 부르다	sing a song
놀라다	be surprised
놓고 가다	leave behind
놓치다	miss
누르다	press
눈을 뜨다	open one's eyes
눈을 붙이다	sleep
눈치를 채다	notice
느끼다	feel
느낌이 나다	feel

ㄷ

다가가다	approach, go closer
다가오다	come closer
다녀오다	go and come back
다루다	treat
다리를 꼬다	cross one's legs
닥치다	shut up, approach
단추를 채우다	fasten a button
달리다	run
담그다	soak
당기다(땡기다)	crave, pull
던지다	throw

덤비다	pick a fight
도망가다	run away
도망치다	run away
돈을 꾸다	borrow money
돈을 빌리다	borrow money
돌이켜 보다	look back
되돌리다	restore
두고가다	leave behind
두근거리다	pound
두리번거리다	look around
뒹굴거리다	laze around
드럼을 치다	play dram
들리다	hear
들어가다	go in
들어오다	come in
들키다	get busted
따르다	follow
땀이 나다	sweat
때려 치우다	quit
떠오르다	float
떨어지다	fall
떼다	take off

ㅁ

마르다	dry
마음에 들다	like
망가지다	be destroyed
망설이다	hesitate
맞추다	set, adjust
머리를 자르다	get a hair cut
머리를 하다	do one's hair
머뭇거리다	hesitate
멈추다	stop
면허를 따다	get a license
모자를 쓰다	wear a cap

문제를 내다	give a question
문지르다	rub
물이 새다	water leaks
물이 흐르다	water flows

ㅂ

바가지를 씌우다	scam
바가지를 쓰다	get scammed
바꾸다	change, switch
바라다	wish, hope
바람을 피우다	cheat on, have an affair
박수를 치다	applaud
받아들이다	accept
받아 주다	accept for
방귀를 뀌다	fart
버스를 타다	get on a bus
버튼을 누르다	press button
버티다	hold out
벗어나다	get out of
벨을 누르다	press the bell
병마개를 따다	pull out a top
보여주다	show
보이다	be seen
보채다	whine
부러지다	be broken
부수다	break, smash
비리다	fishy
비비다	rub
비키다	step aside, move
비행기를 타다	get on a plane
빠져나오다	escape
빠시다	fall out
빨래를 개다	fold the laundry
빼다	take out
뿌리다	sprinkle

No받침 Verbs

ㅅ

사기를 당하다	be scammed
사기를 치다	swindle
사라지다	disappear
산에 오르다	climb a mountain
살아남다	survive
삼키다	swallow
상처가 나다	get hurt
생각이 나다	remember
설레다	be excited
세우다	stand up
소문을 내다	spread a rumor
소문이 퍼지다	a rumor spreads
소화가 되다	digest
숨을 쉬다	breathe
시간이 지나다	time goes by
시리다	cold
시원하다	cool
시키다	make somebody work
신경을 쓰다	take care of
신나다	get excited
싸다	pack
쏘다	shoot
쓰다	use, write
쓰라리다	sore
쓰러지다	collapse
쓰레기를 버리다	dump trash
쓸모없다	useless

ㅇ

아끼다	save
안경을 쓰다	wear glasses
알려 주다	inform
애를 쓰다	make an effort
약속을 지키다	keep one's promise
어울리다	get along with, match
언급하다	mention
얼굴을 가리다	cover one's face
없애다	remove
엉키다	get tangled
연차를 내다	make an annual holiday
영향을 끼치다	cause influence
오타가 나다	type wrong
오타를 내다	be typed wrong
올라가다	go up
올라오다	come up
올리다	put up, upload
욕심나다	be greedy
욕심내다	be greedy
용기가 나다	gather up courage
용기를 내다	be brave
우기다	persist
우산을 펴다	open an umbrella
움직이다	move
월차를 내다	take a monthly holiday
음식을 가리다	be picky about food
일어나다	get up, happen

ㅈ

자물쇠를 잠그다	lock the locker
자빠지다	fall down
자빠트리다	make somebody fall down
잠이 오다	feel sleepy
장난치다	play with
쥐다	hold
지어내다	make up
지우다	erase
지치다	be exhausted
지켜보다	watch
지키다	guard
지하철을 타다	get on the subway
질서를 지키다	keep order

짐을 싸다	pack luggage		필름이 끊기다	black out
찌다	steam			
쪼개다	split		**ㅎ**	
쫓겨나다	be kicked out		한턱내다	treat
ㅊ			한숨을 쉬다	sigh
차다	kick, be full		헷갈리다	be confused
찾아가다	(go) visit, pick up		혼나다	be scolded
찾아오다	(come) visit		흐르다	flow
채우다	fill in		흔들리다	shake
챙기다	take		힘을 내다	cheer up
치다	hit		힘을 빼다	loosen up
치우다	tidy up		힘을 쓰다	use strength
침을 삼키다	swallow saliva		힘을 주다	give strength
ㅋ			힘이 나다	release energy
켜다	turn on			
큰일나다	get into trouble			
ㅌ				
태어나다	be born			
터지다	burst			
튀기다	fry			
틀리다	wrong			
ㅍ				
팔짱을 끼다	cross one's arms			
퍼지다	spread			
펴다	unfold			
펼치다	unfold			
폐를 끼치다	bother			
표를 끊다	buy a ticket			
표를 사다	buy a ticket			
피아노를 치다	play the piano			
피해를 주다	take a toll			

받침 Verbs

ㄱ

가격을 깎다	cut prices
가라앉다	sink
가로막다	block
갈다	change, replace
감각이 있다	have a sense
감기가 낫다	recover from a cold
갚다	pay back
겪다	experience
굽다	bake, roast, grill
긁다	scratch
까먹다	forget
까불다	act up
깨닫다	realize
깨물다	bite
껴입다	wear extra clothing
꼬집다	pinch
꽂다	stick
끈을 풀다	untie a string
끊다	cut off

ㄴ

나이가 들다	get older
나이를 먹다	grow old
남다	be left
낫다	recover, get better
넘다	over, exceed
넣다	put in
녹다	melt
눈을 감다	close one's eyes
눕다	lie down
느낌이 들다	feel

ㄷ

다듬다	trim
다리를 떨다	shake one's leg

ㄷ

다리를 풀다	stretch one's legs
닮다	resemble
담다	put in
닿다	touch
댓글을 달다	write a comment
덮다	cover
도둑이 들다	thief enters
도둑맞다	get stolen
뒤집다	flip
들다	lift
따라잡다	catch up
떨다	shake
뚫다	pierce
뛰어넘다	jump over
뜯다	pluck

ㅁ

마무리짓다	finalize
막다	block
말다	roll
말을 놓다	talk using the familiar form
머리를 감다	wash one's hair
머리를 빗다	brush one's hair
모자를 벗다	take off one's hat
목숨을 걸다	risk one's life
문제를 풀다	solve a question
묻다	ask
밀다	push

ㅂ

바람이 불다	wind blows
바지를 입다	wear pants
발톱을 깎다	cut one's toenails
벗다	take off
볶다	fry

불다	blow
붙다	stick
비웃다	mock
비틀다	twist
빨다	wash, suck
빨래를 걷다	bring in the laundry
빨래를 널다	hang the wash
빼앗다	take
뽑다	pick, pluck

ㅅ

상관없다	no matter
생각이 들다	think of
섞다	mix
속다	be deceived
손톱을 깎다	clip one's nails
수다를 떨다	chatter
숨다	hide
식다	cool down
신발을 벗다	take off shoes
신발을 신다	wear shoes
쌓다	stack
썰다	chop
쏟다	spill
쓰다듬다	pet
쓰레기를 줍다	pick up trash
씹다	chew

ㅇ

아물다	heal
안경을 벗다	take off glasses
양말을 벗다	take off socks
양말을 신다	wear socks
어금니를 깨물다	bite molar
얼다	freeze

엎다	turn over
옷을 벗다	take off clothes
옷을 입다	wear clothes
우산을 접다	fold an umbrella
이를 닦다	brush one's teeth
익다	ripen
입을 다물다	shut one's mouth

ㅈ

자물쇠를 풀다	unlock
잡다	hold, catch, grasp
젖다	get wet
줄다	decrease
줍다	pick up
짐을 풀다	unpack
짓다	build
짖다	bark
쫓다	chase

ㅊ

철이 들다	be mature
철이 없다	be immature
충격을 받다	be shocked
침을 뱉다	spit

ㅋ

| 코드를 꽂다 | plug in a cord |
| 코를 풀다 | blow one's nose |

ㅌ

| 털다 | dust off |
| 틀다 | turn on |

ㅍ

| 풀다 | untie |

하다 Verbs

ㄱ

가입하다	join
간직하다	keep
감동하다	be touched
거짓말하다	lie
검색하다	search
결제하다	pay
경험하다	experience
계산하다	calculate
계속하다	continue
고민하다	worry
고백하다	confess
고생하다	face hardship
고정하다	fix
공감하다	sympathize
공사하다	construct
공지하다	announce
관광하다	go sightseeing
구분하다	divide
구속하다	imprison
구하다	save
극복하다	overcome
금연하다	quit smoking
기대하다	expect
기도하다	pray
기록하다	record
기분이 상하다	offend
기억하다	remember
기절하다	pass out
기침하다	cough
김장하다	make kimchi
깜빡하다	forget

ㄴ

납치하다	kidnap
납부하다	pay (for tax)

낭비하다	waste
너무하다	too bad
노력하다	make an effort

ㄷ

당하다	suffer
당황하다	embarrassed
대신하다	substitute
대여하다	rent
대충하다	wing
대피하다	evacuate
대화하다	converse
대화를 나누다	have a conversation
더하다	add
따라하다	follow
따로따로하다	do separately

ㅁ

마련하다	prepare
마무리하다	finish, complete
만족하다	be satisfied
망하다	fail
면도하다	shave
모집하다	recruit

ㅂ

반말하다	speak impolitely
반응하다	react
발견하다	discover
발전하다	develop
발표하다	announce
방해하다	interrupt
보관하다	store, keep
보호하다	protect
복사하다	copy

부탁하다	ask a favor	연기하다	act, perform
불합격하다	fail (the test)	연애하다	date
비교하다	compare	염려하다	have something on one's mind
		예측하다	predict

ㅅ

		오해하다	misunderstand
사양하다	decline	요구하다	ask for
사정하다	beg	요청하다	request
살살하다	take it easy	욕하다	curse
사과하다	apologize	완료하다	complete
사냥하다	hunt	완성하다	complete
상담하다	counsel	원하다	want
상상하다	imagine	응답하다	reply
상하다	spoil	인증하다	certify
새차하다	wash a car	입양하다	adopt
생각하다	think	입학하다	enter school
생활하다	live, make a living	의식하다	be conscious
세수하다	wash one's face	외식하다	eat out
선언하다	declare		
선택하다	choose		

ㅈ

설득하다	persuade	자극하다	stimulate
설명하다	explain	자살하다	suicide
신청하다	sign up	자제하다	abstain
실망하다	be disappointed	자퇴하다	drop out of school
실수하다	make a mistake	잘난척하다	show off
실천하다	put something into action	잘못하다	do wrong
심행하다	implement	재채기를 하다	sneeze
		저장하다	store
		적응하다	adapt

ㅇ

안내하다	guide	전하다	tell, convey
애원하다	beg	점검하다	inspect
약속하다	promise	접수하다	register
양보하다	yield	정리하다	tidy up
양치하나	brush one's teeth	정색하다	have a serious look
연결하다	connect	제거하다	remove
연구하다	research	제모하다	wax, shave

하다 Verbs

제안하다	suggest		탈락하다	be eliminated
제압하다	overpower		탈출하다	escape
조심하다	be careful		탈퇴하다	leave
조절하다	control, adjust, regulate		탑승하다	board (a plane)
존경하다	respect		탓하다	blame
존재하다	exist		통하다	go through
주문하다	order		퇴근하다	get off work
주의하다	beware		투표하다	vote
주장하다	insist		트림을 하다	burp
지속하다	continue			
지원하다	support		**ㅍ**	
진정하다	calm down			
질투하다	be jealous		파괴하다	destroy
집중하다	concentrate		표현하다	express
집착하다	be obsessed		피하다	avoid
			포장하다	wrap
ㅊ 			폭발하다	explode
참가하다	participate		**ㅎ**	
차별하다	discriminate			
착각하다	be mistaken		하품을 하다	yawn
참견하다	interfere		합격하다	pass (exam)
참고하다	refer		해결하다	solve
참여하다	join in		협박하다	threaten
최선을 다하다	do one's best		화해하다	make up (reconcile)
추가하다	add		환승하다	transfer
추측하다	guess		환영하다	welcome
축하하다	congratulate		환전하다	exchange (money)
출근하다	go to work		획득하다	obtain
출퇴근하다	commute		휴학하다	take time off (from school)
충고하다	advise			
충전하다	charge			
취하다	be drunk			
치료하다	cure			
침범하다	intrude			
체험하다	experience			

받침 Adjectives

ㄱ

가볍다	light
가소롭다	laughable
까다롭다	picky
간지럽다	itchy
갑작스럽다	sudden
경이롭다	phenomenal
괴롭다	painful
귀찮다	not feel like it
깊다	deep
끄떡없다	intact

ㄴ

놀랍다	wonderful

ㄷ

달다	sweet
당황스럽다	unexpected
덥다	hot
드물다	rare
따갑다	sting
뜨겁다	hot

ㅁ

맵다	spicy
목소리가 좋다	have a sweet voice
무겁다	heavy
미끄럽다	slippery

ㅂ

밝다	bright
부끄럽다	ashamed
부담스럽다	uncomfortable
부드럽다	soft
부럽다	envy
부질없다	futile, not worth

ㅅ

사납다	violent
사랑스럽다	adorable
상태가 안 좋다	be in bad condition
상태가 좋다	be in good condition
수치스럽다	shameful
시끄럽다	loud
신비롭다	marvelous
싱겁다	bland

ㅇ

아깝다	a waste, a shame
아름답다	beautiful
아쉽다	feel sorry
안타깝다	feel bad
얕다	shallow
어둡다	dark
어른스럽다	mature
어지럽다	dizzy

ㅈ

자랑스럽다	proud
자연스럽다	natural
조심스럽다	careful
정의롭다	righteous
지겹다	sick and tired
지혜롭다	wise

ㅊ

차갑다	cold
춥다	cold

ㅍ

평화롭다	peaceful

ㅎ

힘들다	hard

하다 Adjectives

ㄱ

개운하다	feel refreshed
건강하다	healthy
깔끔하다	neat, tidy
깜찍하다	cute, dinky
꼼꼼하다	meticulous
깨끗하다	clean
끔찍하다	terrible
귀하다	precious
귀중하다	valuable

ㄴ

나른하다	drowsy
난감하다	be at a loss
넉넉하다	sufficient
느끼하다	oily

ㄷ

단정하다	neat, tidy
답답하다	stuffy
당당하다	confident
대단하다	great
대범하다	big-minded
독특하다	unusual
따뜻하다	warm
딱하다	pathetic
딱딱하다	hard

ㅁ

만만하다	pushover
명랑하다	cheerful
무난하다	easy, safe
무안하다	ashamed
미세하다	tiny
미지근하다	lukewarm
민감하다	sensitive

민망하다	embarrassed

ㅂ

부족하다	lack
불리하다	disadvantageous
불쌍하다	pitiful, poor
불안하다	anxious
불편하다	inconvenient
뻐근하다	stiff
비슷하다	similar

ㅅ

사소하다	trivial
살벌하다	combative
상쾌하다	feel fresh
서늘하다	chilly
서운하다	feel hurt
선명하다	vivid
선하다	nice (personality)
성실하다	faithful
소심하다	timid
소중하다	precious
속상하다	upset
수월하다	easy
순수하다	innocent
순진하다	naive
순하다	mild
시시하다	dull
신기하다	marvelous
신비하다	mysterious
심심하다	bored
신선하다	fresh
심하다	severe
싸늘하다	chilly
쌀쌀하다	chilly

ㅇ

악하다	evil
안전하다	safe
애매하다	ambiguous
어마어마하다	immense
어색하다	awkward
억울하다	feel victimized
연하다	light
예민하다	keen
온순하다	meek
완벽하다	perfect
유리하다	advantageous
익숙하다	be used to

ㅈ

자상하다	attentive
적당하다	moderate
조그마하다	small, little, tiny
지긋지긋하다	be fed up with
지저분하다	messy
진지하다	serious
진하다	thick, dark
짜릿하다	thrilling

ㅊ

충분하다	enough

ㅋ

쾌활하다	cheery

ㅌ

특별히다	special
특이하다	unique

ㅍ

편안하다	comfortable

ㅎ

허전하다	feel empty
현명하다	wise
확실하다	sure
황당하다	absurd
훌륭하다	excellent
흔하다	common

Answers

Unit 1

1
1) 있나요?
2) 맞나요?
3) 예약하나요?
4) 배달하나요?
5) 없나요?
6) 무나요?
7) 운전하나요?
8) 영업하나요?

2
1) 예약하나요?
2) 있나요?
3) 영업하나요?

3
1) 구했나요?
2) 놓쳤나요?
3) 끝났나요?
4) 알아들었나요?
5) 말랐나요?
6) 잡았나요?
7) 시작했나요?
8) 이해했나요?

4
1) 끝났나요?
2) 알아들었나요?
3) 구했나요?

5
1) 납부해야 되나요?
2) 내야 되나요?
3) 송금해야 되나요?
4) 결제해야 되나요?
5) 제출해야 되나요?
6) 입금해야 되나요?

6
1) 제출해야 되나요?
2) 납부해야 되나요?
3) 결제해야 되나요?

Unit 2

1
1) 짠가요?
2) 매운가요?
3) 단가요?
4) 달콤한가요?
5) 신가요?
6) 싱거운가요?
7) 쓴가요?
8) 신선한가요?

2
1) 매운가요?
2) 단가요?

3
1) 직장인인가요?
2) 활발한가요?
3) 청순한가요?

4
1) 영국 사람인가요, 미국 사람인가요?
2) 대학생인가요, 직장인인가요?
3) 키가 큰가요, 키가 작은가요?
4) 활발한가요, 조용한가요?
5) 청순한가요, 섹시한가요?

Unit 3

1
1) 어른일까요?
2) 아이일까요?
3) 쉬울까요?
4) 어려울까요?
5) 클까요?
6) 작을까요?
7) 팔까요?
8) 맞을까요?

2
1) 팔까요?
2) 클까요?
3) 어려울까요?
4) 올까요?
5) 좋을까요?

3
1) 학생일까요, 아저씨일까요?
2) 한국인일까요, 외국인일까요?
3) 잘 어울릴까요, 안 어울릴까요?
4) 쉬울까요, 어려울까요?
5) 열까요, 닫을까요?

Unit 4

1

1) 들킬까 봐
2) 걸릴까 봐
3) 떨어질까 봐
4) 잊어버릴까 봐
5) 잡힐까 봐
6) 놓칠까 봐
7) 맞출까 봐
8) 잃어버릴까 봐
9) 혼날까 봐
10) 망칠까 봐
11) 망가뜨릴까 봐
12) 떨어뜨릴까 봐

2

1) 잡힐까 봐 도망가요.
2) 놓칠까 봐 뛰었어요.
3) 잊어버릴까 봐 메모를 했어요.
4) 더울까 봐 반바지를 입고 왔어요.
5) 떨어질까 봐 공부해요.

3

1) 혼날까 봐
2) 떨어뜨릴까 봐
3) 늦을까 봐
4) 잃어버릴까 봐
5) 떨어질까 봐

Unit 5

1

1) 어린 척하지 마세요.
2) 멋있는 척하지 마세요.
3) 잘생긴 척하지 마세요.
4) 괜찮은 척하지 마세요.
5) 잘난 척하지 마세요.
6) 지친 척하지 마세요.

2

1) 어린 척하세요.
2) 바쁜 척하세요.
3) 괜찮은 척하세요.
4) 배고픈 척하세요.
5) 잘생긴 척하세요.
5) 안 아픈 척하세요.

3

1) 못 알아듣는 척할 거예요.
2) 모르는 척할 거예요.
3) 못 하는 척할 거예요.
4) 마음에 드는 척할 거예요.
5) 잘 못하는 척할 거예요.
6) 잘하는 척할 기예요.

4

1) 일하는 척해야 돼요.
2) 잘하는 척해야 돼요.
3) 모르는 척해야 돼요.
4) 아는 척해야 돼요.
5) 없는 척해야 돼요.
6) 못버는 척해야 돼요.

5

1) 마음에 든 척 했어요.
2) 못 들은 척했어요.
3) 못 본 척했어요.
4) 못 알아들은 척했어요.
5) 모른 척했어요.
6) 잠이 든 척했어요.

6

1) 못 알아들은 척했어요.
2) 못 들은 척했어요.
3) 못 본 척했어요.

Unit 6

1

1) 속을 뻔했어요.
2) 기절할 뻔했어요.
3) 부딪칠 뻔했어요.
4) 까먹을 뻔했어요.
5) 떨어뜨릴 뻔했어요.
6) 사고가 날 뻔했어요.

3

1) 사기를 당할 뻔했어요.
2) 혼날 뻔했어요.
3) 쓰러질 뻔했어요.
4) 넘어질 뻔했어요.
5) 실수할 뻔했어요.
6) 후회할 뻔했어요.
7) 놓칠 뻔했어요.
8) 쏟을 뻔했어요.
9) 합격할 뻔했어요.

Unit 7

1

1) 구입하기로 했어요
2) 그만두기로 했어요
3) 이직하기로 했어요
4) 대신하기로 했어요
5) 휴직하기로 했어요
6) 복직하기로 했어요

3

1) 복수하기로 결정했어요
2) 말을 놓기로 결정했어요
3) 거래하기로 결정했어요
4) 이혼하기로 결정했어요
5) 약혼하기로 결정했어요
6) 결혼하기로 결정했어요

5

1) 돈을 갚기로 약속했어요
2) 버티기로 약속했어요
3) 돌보기로 약속했어요
4) 정신을 차리기로 약속했어요
5) 노력하기로 약속했어요
6) 관리하기로 약속했어요

Unit 8

1

1) 가던 곳
2) 살던 데
3) 쓰던 것
4) 팔던 물건
5) 일하던 회사
6) 사귀던 여자
7) 다니던 교회
8) 사용하던 도구

2

1) 다니던 학교
2) 일하시던 회사/일하던 회사
3) 사귀던 사람

3

1) 쓰던 것
2) 먹던 것
3) 하던 일

4

1) 다녔던 학원
2) 왔던 곳
3) 사셨던 아파트/살던 아파트

Unit 9

1

1) 다녔었어요
2) 사귀었었어요
3) 평범했었어요
4) 근무했었어요
5) 신중했었어요
6) 고집이 셌었어요
7) 꼼꼼했었어요
8) 알바했었어요
9) 잘했었어요
10) 털털했었어요
11) 소심했었어요
12) 까다로웠었어요

2

1) 유치원에 다닐 때 사귀었었어요.
2) 스무 살 때 잘했었어요.
3) 어릴 때 고집이 셌었어요.
4) 사업할 때 돈을 벌었었어요.
5) 젊을 때 인기가 많았었어요.

3

1) 잘했었는데
2) 많았었는데
3) 까다로웠었는데
4) 유명했었는데
5) 못 먹었었는데

Unit 10

1

1) 순하던데요?
2) 사납던데요?
3) 정직하던데요?
4) 청순하던데요?
5) 알던데요?
6) 모르던데요?
7) 복잡하던데요?
8) 순진하던데요?

2

1) 사납던데요?
2) 정직하던데요?
3) 아시던데요?/알던데요?
4) 비가 내리던데요?
5) 학교에 있던데요?

3

1) 청소하고 있던데요?
2) 숙제하고 있던데요?
3) 정리하고 있던데요?
4) 치우고 있던데요?
5) 올라가고 있던데요?
6) 내려가고 있던데요?
7) 기다리고 있던데요?
8) 훔쳐보고 있던데요?
9) 올리고 있던데요?

Unit 11

1

1) 긍정적이더라고요
2) 부정적이더라고요
3) 감동적이더라고요
4) 부드럽더라고요
5) 부끄럽더라고요
6) 어울리더라고요
7) 부럽더라고요
8) 헷갈리더라고요
9) 평화롭더라고요

2

1) 평화롭더라고요
2) 감동적이더라고요
3) 부럽더라고요
4) 긍정적이더라고요
5) 헷갈리더라고요

3

1) 2
2) 1
3) 5
4) 4
5) 3

4

1) 끝났더라고요
2) 가입해야 되더라고요
3) 가고 싶더라고요
4) 보고 있더라고요
5) 비싼 것 같더라고요

Unit 12

1

1) 울어도
2) 졸라도
3) 빌어도
4) 줘도
5) 돈을 벌어도
6) 느려도
7) 어려워도
8) 안 되도
9) 노력해도
10) 졸려도
11) 괴로워도
12) 게을러도

2

1) 비가 내려도
2) 느려도
3) 살아도
4) 있어도
5) 노력해도
6) 어려워도
7) 빌어도
8) 졸라도
9) 안 돼도
10) 줘도

3

1) 늦어도
2) 없어도
3) 기분이 나빠도
4) 잘해 줘도
5) 죽어도

Unit 13

1

1) 부럽지도 않다
2) 부끄럽지도 않다
3) 건드리지도 않다
4) 떨지도 않다
5) 도망가지도 않다
6) 익숙하지도 않다
7) 지겹지도 않다
8) 생각하지도 않다
9) 인정하지도 않다

2

1) 지겹지도 않아요?
2) 인정하지도 않아요.
3) 부끄럽지도 않아요?
4) 익숙하지도 않아요.
5) 건드리지도 않았어요.
6) 떨지도 않네요!
7) 생각하지도 않았어요.
8) 부럽지도 않아요?

4

1) 말하지도 못하다
2) 꿈을 이루지도 못하다
3) 떠들지도 못하다
4) 움직이지도 못하다
5) 가입하지도 못하다
6) 탈퇴하지도 못하다
7) 표현하지도 못하다
8) 손톱을 깎지도 못하다
9) 발톱을 깎지도 못하다

Unit 14

1

1) 외롭더라도
2) 그립더라도
3) 쑥쓰럽더라도
4) 자존심이 상하더라도
5) 힘들더라도
6) 귀찮더라도
7) 이용하더라도
8) 답답하더라도
9) 지겹더라도
10) 화가 나더라도
11) 헤어지더라도
12) 실패하더라도

2

1) 쉽더라도
2) 자존심이 상하더라도
3) 귀찮더라도
4) 화가 나더라도
5) 힘들더라도

Unit 15

1

1) 세우더니
2) 일어서더니
3) 흔들리더니
4) 부르더니
5) 들어오더니
6) 흐려지더니
7) 멈추더니
8) 꺼지더니
9) 건너더니
10) 소리를 지르더니
11) 떨어지더니
12) 다가오더니

2

1) 멈추더니
2) 꺼지더니
3) 다니더니
4) 일어서더니
5) 소리를 지르더니

3

1) 흐려지더니 비가 내리기 시작했어요.
2) 들어오시더니 소리를 지르기 시작했어요.
3) 다가오더니 영어로 질문하기 시작했어요.
4) 흔들리더니 물건들이 떨어지기 시작했어요.
5) 차를 세우더니 다가오기 시작했어요.

Unit 16

1

1) 멀어졌어요
2) 가까워졌어요
3) 깔끔해졌어요
4) 삐뚤어졌어요
5) 부드러워졌어요
6) 딱딱해졌어요
7) 편해졌어요
8) 불편해졌어요
9) 나아졌어요

3

1) 익숙해질 거예요
2) 달라질 거예요
3) 같아질 거예요
4) 밝아질 거예요
5) 어두워질 거예요
6) 복잡해질 거예요
7) 심각해질 거예요
8) 따뜻해질 거예요
9) 차가워질 거예요

4

1) 희미해진 것 같아요
2) 어색해진 것 같아요
3) 빨라진 것 같아요
4) 친해진 것 같아요
5) 흔해진 것 같아요
6) 느려진 것 같아요
7) 소홀해진 것 같아요
8) 까칠해진 것 같아요
9) 진지해진 것 같아요

Unit 17

1

1) 언제인지/언젠지
2) 어디인지/어딘지
3) 누구인지/누군지
4) 무엇인지/뭔지
5) 왜인지/왠지
6) 얼마인지/얼만지
7) 노래인지/노랜지
8) 제목인지
9) 소리인지/소린지
10) 의미인지/의민지

2

1) 언제인지 알아요?
2) 누구인지 기억나요?
3) 어디인지 알고 싶어요?
4) 뭔지 알아요?
5) 무슨 의미인지 물어봐도 돼요?
6) 무슨 노래인지 알아요?
7) 말인지 모르겠어요
8) 인터넷에서 얼마인지 찾아 봤어요?

3

1) 끝나는지

2) 사는지

3) 만나는지

4) 확인하는지

5) 하는지

6) 파는지

7) 구하는지

8) 기록하는지

9) 보고하는지

10) 말하는지

4

1) 몇 시에 끝나는지 알아요?

2) 어디에서 사는지 관심없어요

3) 어디에서 파는지

4) 이걸 왜 좋아하는지 생각해 봤어요?

5) 뭘 좋아하는지 몰랐어요

6) 지금 뭘 하고 있는지 궁금해요

5

1) 왜 여기에 왔는지 알아요?

2) 오늘 뭘 했는지 기록했어요?

3) 어디에서 구했는지 알려 줄래요?

4) 뭘 했는지 보고해야 돼요?

5) 무슨 말을 하셨는지/했는지 들었어요?

6) 무슨 말을 하셨는지/했는지 못 들었어요.

Unit 18

1

1) 첫차인지 막차인지 모르겠어요.

2) 유료인지 무료인지 모르겠어요.

3) 에어컨인지 히터인지 모르겠어요.

4) 사실인지 거짓인지 모르겠어요.

5) 진짜인지 가짜인지 모르겠어요.

2

1) 높은지 낮은지~

2) 좋은지 나쁜지~

3) 위험한지 안전한지~

4) 뜨거운지 차가운지~

5) 큰지 작은지~

3

1) 맞는지 틀리는지~

2) 되는지 안 되는지~

3) 거짓말을 하는지 안 하는지~

4) 파는지 안 파는지~

5) 있는지 없는지~

4

1) 저를 좋아하는지 아닌지 알아야 돼요.

2) 갔는지 몰랐어요.

3) 왔는지 물어볼게요.

4) 이 자켓이 어울리는지 보고 싶어요.

5) 되는지 안 되는지 보여줄 수 있어요?

Unit 19

1

1) 배운 지 얼마나 됐어요?

2) 사귄 지 얼마나 됐어요?

3) 결혼한 지 얼마나 됐어요?

4) 일한 지 얼마나 됐어요?

5) 헤어진 지 얼마나 됐어요?

6) 졸업한 지 얼마나 됐어요?

7) 키운 지 얼마나 됐어요?

8) 임신한 지 얼마나 됐어요?

9) 입원한 지 얼마나 됐어요?

2

1) 한국어를 공부한 지 육 개월 정도 됐어요.

2) 여기에서 산 지 일주일 정도 됐어요.

3) 강아지를 키운 지 십 년 정도 됐어요.

4) 임신한 지 한 달 정도 됐어요.

5) 여행한 지 이틀 정도 됐어요.

5

1) 공부한 지 1년 6개월쯤 됐어요

2) 산 지 2년쯤 됐어요

3) 온 지 2년쯤 되었는데 (됐는데)

Unit 20

1

1) 진짜일지도 몰라요

2) 가짜일지도 몰라요

3) 무료일지도 몰라요

4) 공짜일지도 몰라요

5) 막차일지도 몰라요

6) 귀신일지도 몰라요

7) 천사일지도 몰라요

8) 악마일지도 몰라요

2

1) 가짜일지도 몰라요

2) 공짜일지도 몰라요

3) 악마일지도 몰라요

3

1) 그럴지도 몰라요

2) 면접을 볼지도 몰라요

3) 훔쳐 갈지도 몰라요

4) 큰일 날지도 몰라요

5) 터질지도 몰라요

6) 이사 갈지도 몰라요

7) 들킬지도 몰라요

8) 질투할지도 몰라요

4

1) 면접을 볼지도 몰라요
2) 질투할지도 몰라요
3) 이사 갈지도 몰라요

5

1) 터질지도 모르니까
2) 잡힐지도 모르고
3) 면접을 볼지도 몰라서
4) 훔쳐 갔을지도 몰라요
5) 이사 갈지도 몰라요

Unit 21

1

1) 칭찬인 줄 알다
2) 행운인 줄 알다
3) 휴일인 줄 알다
4) 공짜인 줄 알다
5) 막차인 줄 알다
6) 가죽인 줄 알다
7) 제 것인 줄 알다
8) 동갑인 줄 알다

2

1) 동갑인 줄 알았어요
2) 휴일인 줄 알았어요
3) 제 것인 줄 알았어요

3

1) 친한 줄 알다
2) 가까운 줄 알다
3) 답답한 줄 알다
4) 괜찮은 줄 알다
5) 저렴한 줄 알다
6) 지루한 줄 알다
7) 복잡한 줄 알다
8) 깔끔한 줄 알다

4

1) 복잡한 줄 알았는데
2) 가까운 줄 알았는데
3) 저렴한 줄 알았는데

5

1) 당첨된 줄 알다
2) 뽑힌 줄 알다
3) 다 된 줄 알다
4) 끊긴 줄 알다
5) 결석한 줄 알다
6) 지나친 줄 알다
7) 나은 줄 알다
8) 퇴근한 줄 알다

6

1) 당첨된 줄 알고
2) 다 된 줄 알고
3) 끊긴 줄 알고

Unit 22

1

1) 주인공인 줄 모르다
2) 영화배우인 줄 모르다
3) 방학인 줄 모르다
4) 직원인 줄 모르다
5) 약인 줄 모르다
6) 미성년자인 줄 모르다
7) 외국인인 줄 모르다
8) 주인인 줄 모르다

2

1) 약인 줄 몰랐어요
2) 방학인 줄 몰랐어요
3) 미성년자인 줄 몰랐어요

3

1) 까다로운 줄 모르다
2) 차가운 줄 모르다
3) 가벼운 줄 모르다
4) 대단한 줄 모르다
5) 심각한 줄 모르다
6) 힘든 줄 모르다
7) 무거운 줄 모르다
8) 민감한 줄 모르다

4

1) 무거운 줄 몰랐는데
2) 힘든 줄 몰랐는데
3) 심각한 줄 몰랐는데

5

1) 보낸 줄 모르다
2) 전화가 온 줄 모르다
3) 문자가 온 줄 모르다
4) 그런 줄 모르다
5) 저장한 줄 모르다
6) 주운 줄 모르다
7) 버린 줄 모르다
8) 반납한 줄 모르다

6

1) 보낸 줄 모르고
2) 버린 줄 모르고
3) 문자가 온 줄 모르고

Unit 23

1

1) 만 원이잖아요
2) 주인이잖아요
3) 손님이잖아요
4) 빠르잖아요
5) 느리잖아요
6) 상태가 좋잖아요
7) 변하잖아요
8) 움직이잖아요
9) 따라 하잖아요

2

1) 1,000원이잖아요
2) 주인이잖아요
3) 움직이잖아요
4) 따라 하잖아요
5) 인터넷이 느리잖아요

Unit 24

1

1) 동갑이거든요
2) 대리거든요
3) 과장이거든요
4) 어리거든요
5) 급하거든요
6) 불평하거든요
7) 아름답거든요
8) 예민하거든요
9) 제작하거든요

2

1) 아름답거든요
2) 예민하거든요
3) 제작하거든요

4) 싸거든요
5) 미국 사람이거든요

Unit 25

1

1) 별로인데요?/별론데요?
2) 제 것인데요?/제 건데요?
3) 아직인데요?
4) 처음인데요?

2

1) 제 것인데요?/제 건데요?
2) 별로인데요?/별론데요?
3) 처음인데요?

3

1) 웃긴데요?
2) 진지한데요?
3) 간단한데요?
4) 복잡한데요?

4

1) 진지한데요?
2) 웃긴데요?
3) 복잡한데요?

5

1) 살이 있는데요?
2) 떠나는데요?
3) 움직이는데요?
4) 미는데요?

6

1) 떠나는데요?
2) 움직이는데요?
3) 살아 있는데요?

7

1) 가는데요?
2) 가고 있는데요?
3) 갔는데요?
4) 가야 되는데요?

8

1) 끝났는데요?
2) 못 끝냈는데요?
3) 들어가야 되는데요?

Unit 26

1

1) 듣기
2) 지원하기
3) 합격하기
4) 다루기
5) 키우기
6) 설득하기
7) 설명하기
8) 예측하기
9) 해결하기
10) 선택하기
11) 되돌리기
12) 바꾸기

2

1) 설명하기 힘들어요.
2) 문제를 해결하기 어려워요.
3) 다루기 쉬워요.
4) 말하기는 쉬운데 하기는 힘들어요.
5) 합격하기는 힘든데 지원해 볼게요.

Unit 27

1

1) 필요한 것
2) 큰 것
3) 소중한 것
4) 유용한 것
5) 깨끗한 것
6) 작은 것
7) 쓸모없는 것
8) 차가운 것

2

1) 작은 것이
2) 차가운 것을
3) 쓸모없는 것

3

1) 바라는 것
2) 비용이 드는 것
3) 돈을 버는 것
4) 걱정하는 것
5) 바꾸는 것
6) 갖는 것
7) 인정하는 것
8) 의심하는 것

4

1) 고치는 것은 안 어려운데
비용이 들어요
2) 하는 것은 괜찮은데
위험하니까 조심하세요
3) 돈을 쓰는 것은 쉬운데
버는 것은 힘들어요
4) 인터넷에서 사는 것이 더 저렴해요
5) 버스를 타는 것이 더 빨라요

6) 제가 갖고 싶었던 거예요
7) 제가 바꾼 거예요
8) 제가 못 하는 거예요
9) 제가 잘하는 거예요
10) 제가 사용해도 되는 거예요?

Unit 28

1

1) 외모보다
2) 성격보다
3) 혈액형보다
4) 원숭이보다
5) 금보다
6) 은보다
7) 코끼리보다
8) 운보다
9) 실력보다
10) 시내버스보다
11) 고속버스보다
12) 통학버스보다

3

1) 타는 것보다
2) 갈아타는 것보다
3) 고치는 것보다
4) 주차하는 것보다
5) 올라가는 것보다
6) 내려가는 것보다
7) 수술하는 것보다
8) 모으는 것보다
9) 버는 것보다
10) 선호하는 것보다
11) 내리는 것보다
12) 참는 것보다

Unit 29

1

1) 이런 곳
2) 그런 소리
3) 저런 데
4) 이런 집
5) 그런 말
6) 저런 아이들
7) 이런 사람
8) 그런 표정
9) 저런 것
10) 그런 뜻
11) 어떤 의미
12) 어떤 얘기

2

1) 이런 곳(이런 데)에서 살고 싶어요?
2) 저런 것이(저런 게) 필요해요
3) 저런 사람이랑 놀지 마세요
4) 이런 것을(이런 걸) 좋아해요
5) 이런 것으로(이런 걸로) 해도 돼요?

3

1) 이렇게
2) 그렇게
3) 저렇게

4

1) 이렇게 해야 돼요
2) 저렇게 하고 싶어요
3) 그렇게 하면 힘들어요
4) 저렇게 하지 말고 이렇게 하세요
5) 이렇게 해 보세요

Unit 30

1

1) 낚이다
2) 쌓이다
3) 치이다
4) 베이다
5) 쏘이다
6) 쓰이다
7) 섞이다
8) 깎이다

3

1) 닫히다
2) 막히다
3) 찍히다
4) 뽑히다
5) 잡히다
6) 밟히다
7) 뒤집히다
8) 접히다

5

1) 흔들리다
2) 열리다
3) 걸리다
4) 물리다
5) 밀리다
6) 떨리다
7) 잘리다
8) 눌리다

7

1) 숨기다
2) 끊기다
3) 빼앗기다
4) 벗기다
5) 잠기다
6) 감기다
7) 남기다
8) 안기다

Unit 31

1

1) 승인되다
2) 정리되다
3) 파악되다
4) 설립되다
5) 설치되다
6) 추가되다
7) 사용되다
8) 요구되다
9) 결제되다
10) 취소되다
11) 종료되다
12) 시작되다

3

1) 거절당하다
2) 무시당하다
3) 설득당하다
4) 배신당하다
5) 협박당하다
6) 차별당하다
7) 이용당하다
8) 구타당하다
9) 폭행당하다
10) 사기당하다
11) 해킹당하다
12) 도용당하다

Unit 32

1

1) 퇴사하게 되다
2) 경험하게 되다
3) 퇴원하게 되다
4) 입사하게 되다
5) 감기에 걸리게 되다
6) 입원하게 되다

2

1) 선풍기를 틀고 자서 감기에 걸리게 되었어요.
2) 넘어져서 병원에 입원하게 되었어요.
3) 돈이 없어서 아르바이트를 하게 되었어요.

4

1) 참여하게 되다
2) 사귀게 되다
3) 봉사활동하게 되다
4) 지원하게 되다
5) 말싸움하게 되다
6) 이사 가게 되다

Unit 33

1

1) 떨어져 있다
2) 버려져 있다
3) 새겨져 있다
4) 설치되어 있다
5) 켜져 있다
6) 지정되어 있다
7) 등록되어 있다
8) 깔려 있다
9) 연결되어 있다
10) 서 있다

11) 빠져 있다

12) 매달려 있다

13) 살아 있다

14) 깨져 있다

15) 뽑혀 있다

16) 망가져 있다

2

1) 지정되어

2) 등록되어

3) 연결되어

4) 빠져

5) 떨어져

6) 켜져

7) 깔려

8) 버려져

9) 새겨져

10) 매달려

3

1) 서 있던데요

2) 설치되어 있습니다

3) 뽑혀 있는데요

4) 깨져 있더라고요

5) 망가져 있었어요

Unit 34

1

1) 짜증나게 하다

2) 고민하게 하다

3) 민망하게 하다

4) 놀라게 하다

5) 당황하게 하다

6) 두근거리게 하다

3

1) 곤란하게 만들다

2) 지치게 만들다

3) 착각하게 만들다

4) 난처하게 만들다

5) 당황하게 만들다

6) 설레게 만들다

5

1) 실행시키다

2) 말시키다

3) 배달시키다

4) 심부름시키다

5) 시키다

6) 훈련시키다

Unit 35

1

1) 거칠게

2) 공평하게

3) 화려하게

4) 특별하게

5) 급하게

6) 시시하게

7) 엄격하게

8) 신중하게

9) 꼼꼼하게

10) 튼튼하게

11) 신속하게

12) 간단하게

2

1) 급하게

2) 엄격하게

3) 특별하게

4) 꼼꼼하게

5) 공평하게

6) 재미있게

7) 신속하게

8) 간단하게

9) 신중하게

10) 시시하게

3

1) 엄숙히

2) 우연히

3) 완전히

4) 조용히

5) 정확히

6) 솔직히

7) 편히

8) 과감히

9) 영원히

10) 자세히

11) 분명히

12) 꾸준히

4

1) 천천히

2) 분명히

3) 완전히

4) 꾸준히

5) 자세히

6) 정확히

7) 편히

8) 솔직히

9) 영원히

10) 조용히

Unit 36

1

1) 깊다고요? 얕다고요!

2) 밝다고요? 어둡다고요!

3) 얇다고요? 두껍다고요!

4) 평범하다고요? 특별하다고요!

5) 얕다고요? 깊다고요!

6) 어둡다고요? 밝다고요!

7) 두껍다고요? 얇다고요!

8) 특별하다고요? 평범하다고요!

2

1) 너무 어둡다고요?

2) 다리가 두껍다고요?

3) 귀가 얇다고요?

3

1) 수영을 못 한다고요?

2) 영어를 할 수 있다고요?

3) 지금 운전하고 있다고요?

4) 지금 집에 돌아가야 된다고요?

5) 다 포기하고 싶다고요?

4

1) 자취한대요

2) 금연한대요

3) 포기한대요

4) 자퇴한대요

5) 가입한대요

6) 탈퇴한대요

5

1) 포기한대요

2) 자퇴한대요

3) 금연하신대요/금연한대요

6

1) 가기 싫대요

2) 찍으면 안 된대요

3) 써도 된대요

4) 가지고 와야 된대요

Unit 37

1

1) 넘어졌다고요?

2) 자퇴했다고요?

3) 잡았다고요?

4) 갈아탔다고요?

5) 해결했다고요?

6) 휴학했다고요?

7) 놓쳤다고요?

8) 출발했다고요?

2

1) 새 신발을 샀다고요?

2) 버스를 놓쳤다고요?

3) 1호선으로 갈아탔다고요?

4) 방금 막 출발했다고요?

5) 아르바이트를 시작했다고요?

4

1) 쓰러졌대요

2) 실망했대요

3) 숨었대뇨

4) 떨어트렸대요

5) 실수했대요

6) 나갔대요

7) 속았대요

8) 헤어졌대요

5

1) 떨어트렸대요

2) 나갔대요

3) 실수를 했대요

4) 쓰러졌대요

5) 헤어졌대요

Unit 38

1

1) 던질 거라고요

2) 허전할 거라고요

3) 바꿀 거라고요

4) 보관할 거라고요

5) 갈아탈 거라고요

6) 휴학할 거라고요

7) 자를 거라고요

8) 관리할 거라고요

2

1) 머리를 자를 거라고요?

2) 보관할 거라고요?

3) 지하철을 갈아탈 거라고요?

4) 차를 바꿀 거라고요?

5) 허전할 거라고요?

3

1) 복수할 거래요

2) 글을 올릴 거래요

3) 뽑을 거래요

4) 버릴 거래요

5) 돌아올 거래요

6) 갈아입을 거래요

7) 끊을 거래요

8) 추가할 거래요

4

1) 글을 올릴 거래요
2) 돌아올 거래요 (돌아오실 거래요)
3) 뽑을 거래요
4) 끊을 거래요 (끊으실 거래요)
5) 버릴 거래요 (버리실 거래요)

Unit 39

1

1) 몇 살이냐고요?
2) 무슨 요일이냐고요?
3) 언제냐고요?
4) 뭐냐고요?

2

1) 한국 사람이냐고요?
2) 생일이 언제냐고요?
3) 몇 살이냐고요?
4) 이게 뭐냐고요?

3

1) 같냐고요?
2) 다르냐고요?
3) 틀리냐고요?
4) 맞냐고요?

4

1) 같냐고요?
2) 다르냐고요?
3) 맞냐고요?
4) 틀리냐고요?

5

1) 화장했냐고요?
2) 파마했냐고요?
3) 염색했냐고요?
4) 잘랐냐고요?

6

1) 파마했냐고요?
2) 머리를 잘랐냐고요?
3) 어디에서 염색했냐고요?
4) 오늘 화장했냐고요?

7

1) 어디에 가고 싶냐고요?
2) 내일 출근해야 되냐고요?
3) 뭐를 마실 거냐고요?
4) 뭐 하고 있냐고요?
5) 영어를 할 수 있냐고요?
6) 여기에 와 봤냐고요?

8

1) 친구가 언제 오냐고 해서
제가 내일 간다고 했어요.
2) 남편이 뭐를 하고 싶냐고 해서
집에 있고 싶다고 했어요.
3) 후배가 영국에 가 봤냐고 해서
안 가 봤다고 했어요.

Unit 40

1

1) 몇 시라고요?
2) 막차라고요?
3) 금요일이라고요?
4) 뭐라고요?

2

1) 금요일이라고요?
2) 3시라고요?
3) 막차라고요?
4) 마흔 살이라고요?

3

1) 지우라고요
2) 포기하라고요
3) 시키라고요
4) 치우라고요

4

1) 포기하라고요?
2) 치우라고요!
3) 지우라고요?
4) 동생한테 시키라고요?

5

1) 김밥이라고 해요
2) 갈비라고 해요
3) 삼겹살이라고 해요
4) 비빔밥이라고 해요

6

1) 이라고 해요
2) 라고 해요
3) 이라고 해요
4) 이라고 해요

7

1) 누가 하라고 했어요?
2) 하라고 해야 돼요?
3) 하라고 하세요
4) 하라고 해도 돼요?
5) 하라고 할 거예요
6) 하라고 할 수 있어요?

8

1) 엄마가 대학교에 가라고 해서 갔어요.
2) 아빠가 돈을 쓰지 말라고 해서 모으기
시작했어요.
3) 친구가 먹어 보라고 해서 먹어 봤어요.

9

1) 동생이 오라고 했는데 안 갔어요.

2) 천천히 하라고 했는데 빨리 했어요.

3) 할아버지가 사지 말라고 했는데 샀어요.

Unit 41

1

1) 쉬자고요

2) 줍자고요

3) 훔치자고요

4) 도망가자고요

5) 걷자고요

6) 버리자고요

7) 사귀자고요

8) 헤어지자고요

2

1) 헤어지자고요?

2) 도망가자고요?

3) 쓰레기를 줍자고요?

3

1) 말을 놓재요

2) 포기하재요

3) 도전하재요

4) 반말을 하재요

5) 바꾸재요

6) 기다리재요

4

1) 헤어지재요

2) 반말을 하재요/말을 놓재요

3) 가지 말재유

Unit 42

1

1) 차를 달라고요

2) 여유를 달라고요

3) 용기를 달라고요

4) 희망을 달라고요

5) 표를 달라고요

6) 자신감을 달라고요

7) 일을 달라고요

8) 자유를 달라고요

2

1) 시간을 달라고요?

2) 용기를 달라고요?

3) 희망을 달라고요?

3

1) 말을 걸어 달래요

2) 들어 달래요

3) 켜 달래요

4) 교환해 달래요

5) 꺼 달래요

6) 틀어 달래요

4

1) 꺼 달라고 했어요 (꺼 달랬어요)

2) 켜 달라고 했어요 (켜 달랬어요)

3) 틀어 달라고 했어요 (틀어 달랬어요)

Unit 43

1

1) 봄이라면서요

2) 여름이라면서요

3) 가을이라면서요

4) 겨울이라면서요

2

1) 여름이라면서요?

2) 봄이라면서요?

3

1) 돌아간다면서요

2) 출근한다면서요

3) 퇴근한다면서요

4) 야근한다면서요

4

1) 야근한다면서요?

2) 퇴근한다면서요?

3) 돌아간다면서요?

5

1) 다 했다면서요

2) 찾았다면서요

3) 나갔다면서요

4) 나왔다면서요

6

1) 다 했다면서요?

2) 나왔다면서요?

3) 찾았다면서요?

7

1) 다닐 거라면서요

2) 그만둘 거라면서요

3) 지원할 거라면서요

4) 올릴 거라면서요

8

1) 올릴 기라면서요

2) 다닐 거라면서요

3) 지원할 거라면서요

Unit 44

1

1) 박수를 치면서
2) 피아노를 치면서
3) 춤을 추면서
4) 노래를 부르면서
5) 핸드폰을 보면서
6) 비를 맞으면서
7) 게임하면서
8) 거울을 보면서
9) 다리를 떨면서

2

1) 노래를 들으면서 공부해요.
2) 박수를 치면서 노래를 부르고 있어요.
3) 게임하면서 라면을 먹고 싶어요.
4) 드라마를 보면서 쉴 거예요.
5) 핸드폰을 보면서 횡단보도를 건넜대요.

3

1) 보면서/보시면서
2) 하면서
3) 피우면서/피우시면서
4) 으면서
5) 으면서

Unit 45

1

1) 까불다가
2) 장난치다가
3) 치우다가
4) 욕심을 부리다가
5) 지나가다가
6) 피하다가
7) 비교하다가
8) 고민하다가
9) 사업하다가
10) 따라 하다가
11) 지나가다가
12) 한눈을 팔다가

2

1) 핸드폰을 보면서 걷다가 넘어졌어요.
2) 계단에서 뛰다가 다쳤어요.
3) 버스에서 졸다가 못 내렸어요.
4) 방을 청소하다가 발견했어요.
5) 회사를 다니다가 그만뒀어요.

Unit 46

1

1) 작업하느라
2) 챙기느라
3) 돌보느라
4) 집중하느라
5) 샤워하느라
6) 도와주느라
7) 준비하느라
8) 얘기하느라
9) 생각하느라
10) 밤을 새우느라
11) 내느라
12) 시험을 보느라

2

1) 아기를 돌보느라 정신이 없어요.
2) 이것 저것 생각하느라 늦게 잤어요.
3) 일하느라 바쁠걸요.
4) 샤워하느라 몰랐어요.
5) 시험공부하느라 밤을 새웠어요.

Unit 47

1

1) 욕먹을 만하다
2) 칭찬할 만하다
3) 불평할 만하다
4) 견딜 만하다
5) 참을 만하다
6) 대결할 만하다
7) 질투할 만하다
8) 고민할 만하다
9) 자랑할 만하다
10) 적응할 만하다
11) 지낼 만하다
12) 버틸 만하다

2

1) 불평할 만해요
2) 욕을 먹을 만해요
3) 견딜 만해요
4) 볼 만해요
5) 지낼 만해요

3

1) 가 볼 만해요
2) 도전해 볼 만해요
3) 다녀 볼 만해요
4) 타 볼 만해요
5) 대결해 볼 만해요

Unit 48

1

1) 멀긴 하다/멀긴 멀다
2) 맵긴 하다/맵긴 맵다
3) 짜긴 하다/짜긴 짜다
4) 궁금하긴 하다/궁금하긴 궁금하
5) 고맙긴 하다/고맙긴 고맙다

6) 작긴 하다/작긴 작다

7) 느리긴 하다/느리긴 느리다

8) 부담스럽긴 하다/부담스럽긴 부담
스럽다

2

1) 맵긴 한데

2) 사이즈가 작긴 한데

3) 속도가 느리긴 한데

4) 위험하긴 한데

5) 아프긴 한데

3

1) 느리긴 한데

2) 위험하긴 한데

3) 고맙긴 한데

4) 어렵긴 한데

5) 있긴 한데

4

1) 혼나긴 했는데

2) 먹긴 했는데

3) 숙제를 해야 되긴 하는데

4) 기타를 칠 줄 알긴 하는데

5) 본 적이 있긴 한데

Unit 49

1

1) 쳐다보길래

2) 놀리길래

3) 무시하길래

4) 할인하길래

5) 따라오길래

6) 소리를 지르길래

7) 물어보길래

8) 알려주길래

9) 열이 나길래

10) 기침이 나길래

11) 충동구매하길래

12) 갔다 오길래

2

1) 놀리길래

2) 따라오길래

3) 물어보길래

4) 있길래

5) 없길래

3

1) 열이 나고 기침이 나길래 병
원에 갔다 왔어요.

2) 백화점에서 50%를 할인하길
래 충동구매했어요.

3) 형이 같이 가자고 하길래 따
라갔어요.

4) 멋진 차가 지나가길래 부러워
서 계속 쳐다봤어요.

5) 동생이 저를 무시하길래 소리
를 질렀어요.

Unit 50

1

1) 슬퍼하다

2) 외로워하다

3) 불안해하다

4) 궁금해하다

5) 그리워하다

6) 부담스러워하다

7) 창피해하다

8) 쑥스러워하다

2

1) 그리워해요

2) 부담스러워해요

3) 불안해해요

4) 궁금해해요

5) 외로워해요

6) 슬퍼해요

3

1) 슬퍼해서

2) 궁금해하셔서

3) 창피해하는 것 같아요

4) 그리워할 지도 몰라요

5) 슬퍼하실 테니까

4

1) 따라 하고 싶어 하다

2) 키우고 싶어 하다

3) 바꾸고 싶어 하다

4) 알리고 싶어 하다

5) 복수하고 싶어 하다

6) 빌리고 싶어 하다

7) 배우고 싶어 하다

8) 갖고 싶어 하다

5

1) 배우고 싶어 해요

2) 바꾸고 싶어 해요

3) 갖고 싶어 해요

4) 키우고 싶어 해요

5) 알리고 싶어 해요

6) 되고 싶어 해요

7) 먹고 싶어 해요

8) 내려가고 싶어 하세요

9) 이민가고 싶어 하세요

10) 그만두고 싶어해요

Unit 51

1

1) 숨을 쉴 때마다
2) 제안할 때마다
3) 바람이 불 때마다
4) 어지러울 때마다
5) 하품할 때마다
6) 추가할 때마다
7) 환승할 때마다
8) 상담할 때마다
9) 거절당할 때마다
10) 카드를 찍을 때마다
11) 헷갈릴 때마다
12) 괴로울 때마다

2

1) 제안할 때마다
2) 어지러울 때마다
3) 환승할 때마다
4) 바람이 불 때마다

Unit 52

1

1) 터질 때까지
2) 달성할 때까지
3) 만족할 때까지
4) 이해할 때까지
5) 해가 뜰 때까지
6) 해가 질 때까지
7) 될 때까지
8) 마음에 들 때까지
9) 합격할 때까지
10) 죽을 때까지
11) 답장할 때까지
12) 나올 때까지

Unit 53

1

1) 거짓말일 리가 없다
2) 진짜일 리가 없다
3) 스님일 리가 없다
4) 사실일 리가 없다
5) 가벼울 리가 없다
6) 무거울 리가 없다
7) 뜨거울 리가 없다
8) 차가울 리가 없다
9) 질 리가 없다
10) 알 리가 없다
11) 모를 리가 없다
12) 그럴 리가 없다

2

1) 거짓말일 리가 없어요
2) 진짜일 리가 없어요
3) 싫어할 리가 없어요
4) 12시일 리가 없어요
5) 눈이 내릴 리가 없어요

3

1) 떠났을 리가 없어요
2) 지고 있을 리가 없어요
3) 해 본 적이 없을 리가 없어요
4) 할 수 있을 리가 없어요
5) 오셨을 리가 없어요

Unit 54

1

1) 진행할 수밖에 없다
2) 신고할 수밖에 없다
3) 가입할 수밖에 없다
4) 압수할 수밖에 없다
5) 틀 수밖에 없다
6) 지울 수밖에 없다
7) 탈퇴할 수밖에 없다
8) 그만둘 수밖에 없다
9) 끊을 수밖에 없다
10) 책임질 수밖에 없다
11) 돌아갈 수밖에 없다
12) 추방할 수밖에 없다

2

1) 틀 수 밖에 없어요
2) 가입할 수 밖에 없어요
3) 돌아갈 수 밖에 없어요
4) 책임질 수 밖에 없어요
5) 압수할 수 밖에 없어요

3

1) 끊을 수 밖에 없었어요
2) 그만둘 수 밖에 없었어요
3) 탈퇴할 수 밖에 없었어요
4) 신고할 수 밖에 없었어요
5) 틀 수 밖에 없었어요

Unit 55

1

1) 던져 버리다
2) 잘라 버리다
3) 밀어 버리다
4) 그만둬 버리다
5) 녹아 버리다
6) 차단해 버리다
7) 도망가 버리다
8) 놓쳐 버리다
9) 끊어 버리다
10) 지워 버리다
11) 삭제해 버리다
12) 멈춰 버리다

2

1) 잘라 버렸어요
2) 던져 버렸어요
3) 도망가 버렸어요
4) 놓쳐 버렸어요
5) 밀어 버렸어요

3

1) 직장을 그만둬 버리고 싶어요.
2) 사진을 삭제해 버릴 거예요.
3) 이상한 사람은 차단해 버리세요.
4) 그냥 가 버리면 어떻게 해요.
5) 전화를 끊어 버리는 게 어때요.

Unit 56

1

1) 넣어 놓다
2) 빼 놓다
3) 남겨 놓다
4) 널어 놓다
5) 켜 놓다
6) 꺼 놓다
7) 보관해 놓다
8) 정리해 놓다
9) 맡겨 놓다
10) 치워 놓다
11) 빨래해 놓다
12) 막아 놓다

2

1) 넣어 놓았어요
2) 켜 놓았어요
3) 맡겨 놓았어요
4) 열어 놓았어요
5) 정리해 놓았어요

3

1) 넣어 놓았으니까
2) 다 해 놓았으니까
3) 맡겨 놓았으니까
4) 틀어 놓았으니까
5) 다운로드 해 놓았으니까

Unit 57

1

1) 뛰어 가다
2) 알아 가다
3) 되어 가다 (돼 가다)
4) 완성되어 가다
5) 챙겨 가다
6) 끝나 가다
7) 훔쳐 가다
8) 죽어 가다
9) 지나 가다
10) 사 가다
11) 마무리해 가다
12) 돌아 가다

2

1) 완성되어 가고 있어요
2) 알아 가는 중이에요
3) 잘되어 가요
4) 써 가고 있긴 한데
5) 챙겨 가세요

3

1) 거의 다 해 가니까 조금만 기다려 주세요.
2) 음식이 거의 다 되어 가니까 식탁에 앉으세요.
3) 밤에 추울지도 모르니까 옷을 넉넉히 챙겨 가세요.
4) 새가 날아 갔어요.
5) 위험하니까 뛰어 가지 말고 천천히 가세요.

Unit 58

1

1) 챙겨 오다
2) 연구해 오다
3) 뛰어 오다
4) 걸어 오다
5) 찾아 오다
6) 참가해 오다
7) 싸 오다
8) 키워 오다
9) 사 오다
10) 날아 오다
11) 돌아 오다
12) 생활해 오다

2

1) 챙겨 왔어요
2) 뛰어 왔어요
3) 싸 왔어요
4) 벌어 왔어요
5) 돌아 왔어요

3

1) 노력해 왔는데
2) 연구해 왔습니다
3) 생활해 왔기 때문에
4) 참가해 온 지
5) 훈련해 왔기 때문에

Unit 59

1

1) 챙길 테니까
2) 도와줄 테니까
3) 들 테니까
4) 마무리할 테니까
5) 책임질 테니까
6) 맡을 테니까
7) 갖고 올 테니까
8) 확인할 테니까

2

1) 책임질 테니까
2) 갖고 올 테니까
3) 마무리할 테니까
4) 들 테니까
5) 확인할 테니까

4

1) 알아서 할 텐데
2) 바뀔 텐데
3) 돈이 들 텐데
4) 처리할 텐데
5) 불안할 텐데
6) 답답할 텐데
7) 더러워질 텐데
8) 방해될 텐데

5

1) 알아서 할텐데
2) 될텐데
3) 들텐데
4) 답답할텐데
5) 더러워질텐데

Unit 60

1

1) 맛있겠어요
2) 힘들겠어요
3) 좋겠어요
4) 아프겠어요
5) 미치겠어요
6) 죽겠어요
7) 어렵겠어요
8) 피곤하겠어요

2

1) 피곤하겠어요
2) 좋겠어요
3) 아프겠어요

3

1) 바쁘겠네요
2) 기쁘겠네요
3) 재미있겠네요
4) 시원하겠네요
5) 한가하겠네요
6) 짜증나겠네요
7) 따뜻하겠네요
8) 쌀쌀하겠네요

4

1) 바쁘겠네요
2) 기쁘겠네요
3) 쌀쌀하겠네요

5

1) 종료하겠습니다
2) 드리겠습니다
3) 공개하겠습니다
4) 사과하겠습니다
5) 해결하겠습니다

6) 처리하겠습니다
7) 교육하겠습니다
8) 제출하겠습니다

6

1) 제출하겠습니다
2) 드리겠습니다
3) 처리하겠습니다

Unit 61

1

1) 빠르면 빠를수록
2) 많으면 많을수록
3) 게으르면 게으를수록
4) 밝으면 밝을수록
5) 크면 클수록
6) 작으면 작을수록
7) 높으면 높을수록
8) 낮으면 낮을수록

2

1) 빠르면 빠를수록 좋아요
2) 많으면 많을수록 좋아요
3) 밝으면 밝을수록 좋아요

3

1) 지나면 지날수록
2) 생각하면 할수록
3) 실패하면 할수록
4) 나누면 나눌수록
5) 보면 볼수록
6) 도전하면 할수록
7) 파면 팔수록
8) 숨을 쉬면 쉴수록

4

1) 지나면 지날수록
2) 생각하면 할수록
3) 하면 할수록
4) 나누면 나눌수록
5) 보면 볼수록

Final Test 1

1) C	29) B	57) D	85) A	113) D
2) A	30) C	58) B	86) B	114) B
3) C, C	31) D	59) B	87) D	115) D
4) A, A	32) A	60) A	88) C	116) A
5) B	33) B	61) D	89) D	117) A
6) A, A	34) C	62) A	90) A	118) D
7) C	35) A	63) C	91) C	119) B
8) D	36) C	64) B	92) A	120) B
9) B	37) A	65) B	93) C	121) D
10) B	38) C	66) C	94) D	122) B
11) D	39) D	67) A	95) B	123) B
12) C	40) B	68) B	96) B, C	124) A
13) B	41) C	69) B	97) A	125) A
14) A	42) D	70) A	98) C	126) B
15) B	43) A	71) D	99) B	127) D
16) C	44) A	72) B	100) C	128) A
17) B	45) B	73) B	101) B	129) C
18) B	46) A, A	74) B	102) A	130) B
19) D	47) D, D	75) B	103) B	131) C
20) A	48) C	76) B	104) B	132) B
21) C	49) C	77) C	105) C	133) D
22) A	50) A	78) A	106) D	134) A
23) C	51) D	79) C	107) A	135) B
24) A	52) B	80) C	108) B	136) D
25) B	53) A	81) B	109) C	137) A
26) A	54) B	82) C	110) A	138) B
27) D	55) C	83) B	111) B	139) A
28) C	56) A	84) A	112) C	140) B
				141) C
				142) B

Korean Grammar
for Speaking 2

초판 1쇄	2018. 11. 22
발 행 인	송원
발 행 처	송원
주 소	경기도 수원시 영통구 망포동 691, 104-2304
대표전화	+82 10-8747-1048
출판등록	제2016-000003호
이 메 일	rokmcsw@gmail.com
Website	www.heywon.kr
ISBN	979-11-957162-4-1

First Published	November 22th, 2018
Written by	Song Won
Publisher	Song Won
Address	Mangpo 691, Suwon, Gyunggi, South Korea
Contact Number	+82 10-8747-1048
Publication License	제2016-000003호
Email	rokmcsw@gmail.com
Website	www.heywon.kr
ISBN	979-11-957162-4-1